Simple Psalter

for Year B

J. Michael Joncas

LITURGICAL PRESS
Collegeville, Minnesota

www.litpress.org

ACKNOWLEDGMENTS

Cover design: Tara Wiese. Photo courtesy of Getty Images.

The English translation of Psalm Responses from *Lectionary for Mass* © 1969, 1981, 1997, International Commission on English in the Liturgy Corporation. All rights reserved.

Verse texts from *The Abbey Psalms and Canticles* by the Monks of Conception Abbey, © 2018, 2010, United States Conference of Catholic Bishops. All rights reserved.

© 2023 The Jan Michael Joncas Trust
Published by Liturgical Press, Collegeville, Minnesota. All rights reserved. No part of this book may be used or reproduced in any manner whatsoever except brief quotations in reviews, without the written permission of Liturgical Press, Saint John's Abbey, PO Box 7500, Collegeville, MN 56321-7500. Printed in the United States of America.

ISBN: 978-0-8146-6785-9   ISBN: 978-0-8146-6786-6 (e-book)

Contents

Psalms for feast days and solemnities, such as Christmas and Easter, can be found in *Simple Psalter for Solemnities, Feasts, and Other Celebrations*. Available at www.litpress.org.

Composer's Notes

My "simple psalms" project is intended to help worshiping communities with limited musical resources to sing the appointed Responsorial Psalm for the Sundays and Holydays of the Liturgical Year. I have set the texts as they appear in the English-language *Lectionary for Mass, Second Typical Edition* (1998) (antiphons) and the *Abbey Psalms and Canticles* (verses). All of the antiphons are set metrically (i.e., not in the free rhythm of chant) because I believe that in most cases in the English-speaking world this makes their texts more memorable and easier to sing for the assembly. The verses are set to rhythmic psalm-tones similar to those of Gelineau psalmody (i.e., speech-rhythm settings of the text over pulsed accompaniment ["sprung rhythm"]). Unlike the published Gelineau psalms, however, I have notated the way I propose that the texts to be sung since I find that it is sometimes difficult for cantors to sing the Gelineau tones as notated using only whole notes. A suggested tempo appears at the beginning of each psalm as a metronome mark; this tempo can be adjusted depending on the acoustic properties of the space in which the liturgy is celebrated.

Tones are assigned to each psalm based on the genre (*Gattung*) of the psalm-text, following the pattern of my friend and colleague, Art Zannoni, as follows:

Tone 1A: Hymn of Praise, Motivation from Nature

Tone 1B: Hymn of Praise, Motivation from History or Torah

Tone 1C: Song of Zion

Tone 1D: Processional

Tone 1E: Hymn of Praise to YHWH as King

Tone 2A: Royal Coronation or Anniversary

Tone 2C: Royal Song of Thanksgiving

Tone 2D: Royal Marriage Song

Tone 3: Prophetic Psalm

Tone 4A: Community Lament

Tone 4B: Individual Lament

Tone 4C: Prayer for the Sick

Tone 5A: Communal Thanksgiving

Tone 5B: Individual Thanksgiving

Tone 6: Psalm of Confidence

Tone 8A: Wisdom Psalm 1

Tone 8B: Wisdom Psalm 2

(Missing tone numbers indicate a psalm-genre that does not appear in the Sunday and Solemnity Lectionary.)

I would here like to acknowledge the influence of three church composers whose psalm settings have influenced this project. I have already mentioned Fr. Joseph Gelineau, S.J., whose groundbreaking creation of "pulsed" psalm-tones set to sprung-rhythm texts made one of the metrical characteristics of Hebrew biblical psalms and canticles available for vernacular singing. A second influence was Howard Hughes, S.M., whose assigning of particular tones to particular genres of psalms based in contemporary form-critical analysis of the psalm-texts, has been eye- and ear-opening for me. Finally Paul Inwood was the first to call my attention to the idea of "psalm tunes" (rather than "psalm tones"). He showed how many English-language folk songs adjusted the fundamental melodic curves of their tones, eliding some syllables while assigning multiple notes to a single syllable based on the number of syllables needed.

Following the practice articulated in the *Lectionary for Mass*, these Responsorial Psalms would be performed as follows. After a period of silence to reflect on the previous scriptural reading proclaimed, a keyboard (or melody instrument) would play the melody for the Antiphon alone. The cantor would immediately intone the Antiphon with a keyboard providing accompaniment, if needed. The assembly would then repeat the Antiphon with a keyboard (and optionally other instruments) providing accompaniment, if needed. The cantor would then sing the assigned psalm verses with the assembly repeating the Antiphon after each verse.

While I believe these "simple psalms" can effectively be sung *a cappella* or with simple keyboard accompaniment, some communities might want to enhance their singing of the Responsorial Psalm with more elaborate music.

The optional harmony additions to the antiphons can be performed in a multitude of ways.

Vocally, the harmonies:

1) might be sung by soloists with the rest of the choir singing the antiphon in unison with the assembly.

2) might be sung by the soprano and alto sections of the choir with the men singing the antiphon in unison with the assembly.

3) If an SATB texture is desired, the soprano and bass sections sing the antiphon in unison with the assembly, with the tenors singing the higher harmonies an octave lower than written and the altos singing the lower harmonies as notated.

Instrumentally,

1) the SA harmonies might be played by C treble wind or string instruments, either as notated or an octave higher depending on where it best fits the instruments' tessitura.

2) the keyboardist should keep the pulse constant under the singing of the verses, but might repeat the chords as quarter notes rather than half notes, or even arpeggiate the chords as eighth notes if desired.

My preference is that the Verses be sung by a solo cantorial voice since that seems to ensure that the psalm-text be clearly sung and understood. Most of the time I have set the psalm-text for two phrases on one breath; the cantor should feel free to take a breath at an appropriate place if singing both phrases on one breath is too taxing. It is also possible to alternate male and female solo voices on the Verses, possibly with both singing the final Verse in octaves. It would also be possible to have the choir sing the verses (or just the final Verse) in unison, as long as their articulation keeps the psalm-text intelligible.

As the *Lectionary for Mass* reminds us: "The working of the Holy Spirit is needed if the word of God is to make what we hear outwardly have its effect inwardly. Because of the Holy Spirit's inspiration and support, the word of God becomes the foundation of the liturgical celebration and the rule and support of all our life. The working of the Holy Spirit precedes, accompanies and brings to completion the whole celebration of the Liturgy. But the Spirit also brings home to each person individually everything that in the proclamation of the word of God is spoken for the good of the whole gathering of the faithful" [9]. I pray that my musical settings of these "simple psalms" may help Christ's faithful, individually and collectively, hear the word of God and put it into practice in their lives. *Soli Deo gloria.*

(Fr. Jan) Michael Joncas
St. Paul, MN

Psalm 80: Lord, Make Us Turn to You

First Sunday of Advent, Year B

Ps 80:2-3, 15-16, 18-19

Michael Joncas
Tone 4A: Community Lament

First Sunday of Advent, Year B

First Sunday of Advent, Year B

First Sunday of Advent, Year B

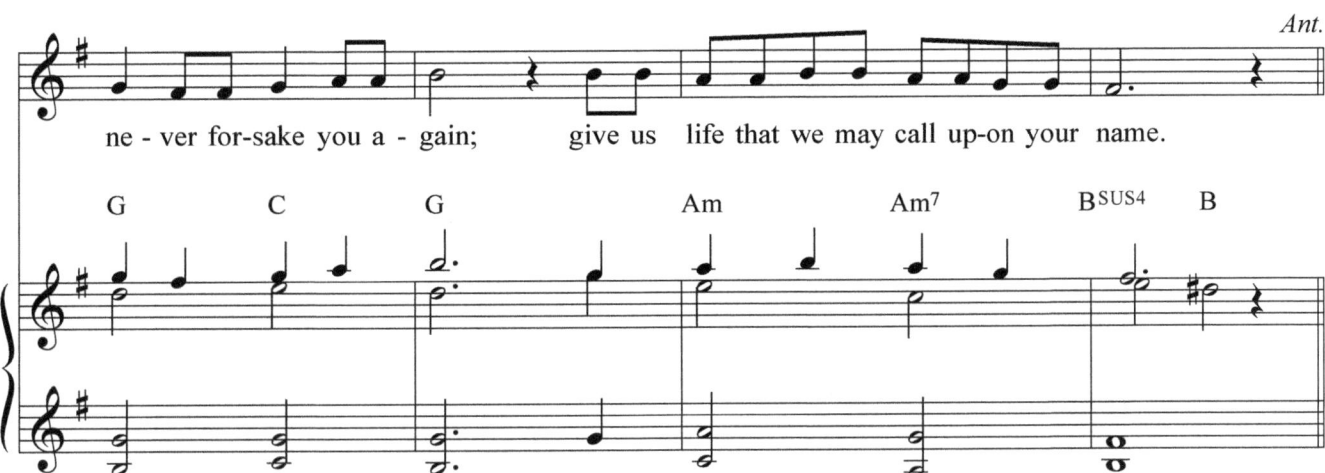

Psalm 85: Lord, Let Us See Your Kindness

Second Sunday of Advent, Year B

Ps 85:9-10, 11-12, 13-14

Michael Joncas
Tone 3: Prophetic Psalm

Second Sunday of Advent, Year B

Second Sunday of Advent, Year B

Canticle of Mary: My Soul Rejoices in My God
Third Sunday of Advent, Year B

Luke 1:46-48, 49-50, 53-54   Michael Joncas

Third Sunday of Advent, Year B

Third Sunday of Advent, Year B

Psalm 89: Forever I Will Sing
Fourth Sunday of Advent, Year B

Ps 89:2-3, 4-5, 27, 29

Michael Joncas
Tone 1E: Hymn of Praise to YHWH as King

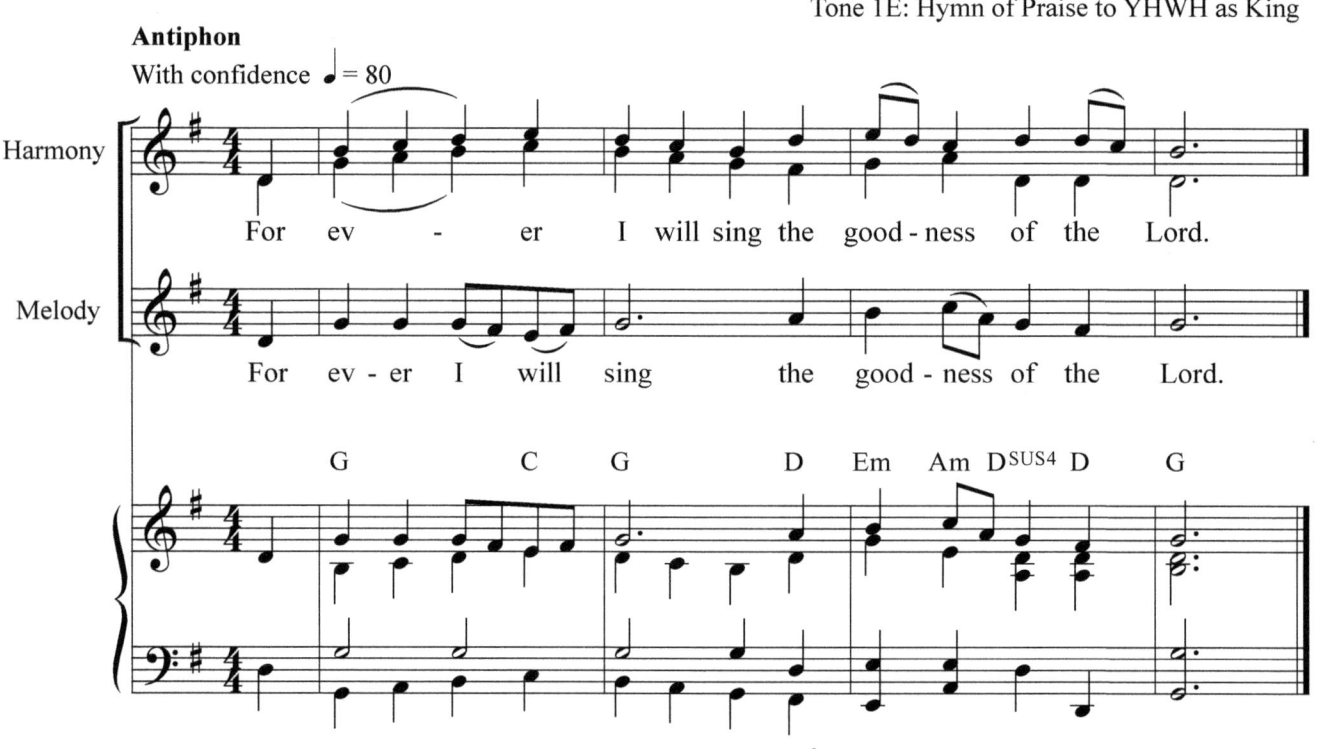

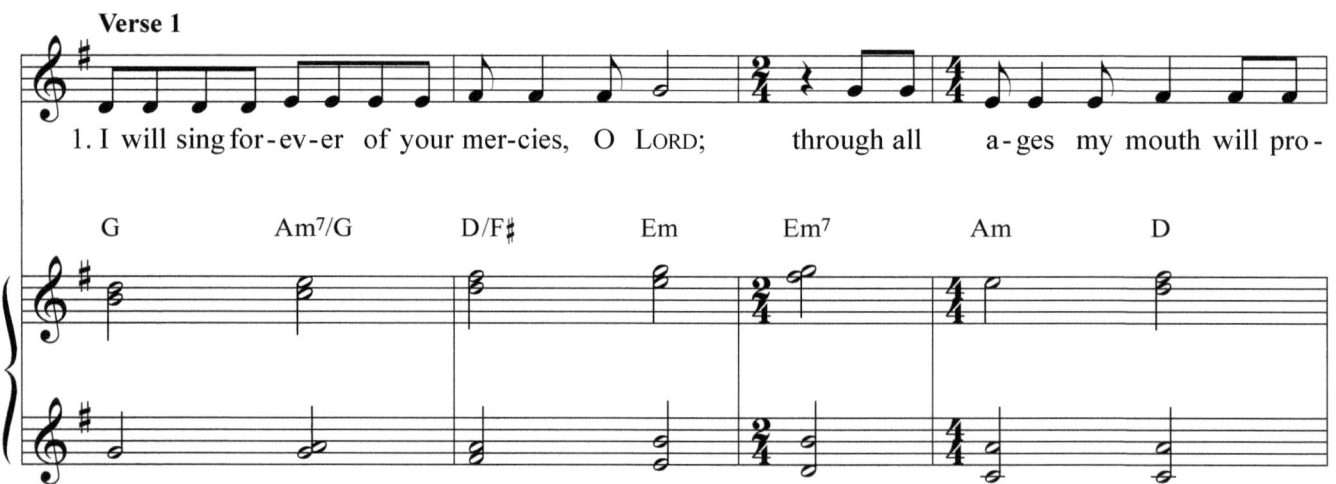

Fourth Sunday of Advent, Year B

Fourth Sunday of Advent, Year B

Fourth Sunday of Advent, Year B

Psalm 25: Your Ways, O Lord, Are Truth and Love
First Sunday of Lent, Year B

Ps 25:4-5, 6, 7, 8-9

Michael Joncas
Tone 8B: Wisdom Psalm 2

First Sunday of Lent, Year B

First Sunday of Lent, Year B

Psalm 116: I Will Walk before the Lord

Second Sunday of Lent, Year B

Ps 116:10, 15, 16-17, 18-19

Michael Joncas
Tone 5B: Individual Thanksgiving

Second Sunday of Lent, Year B

Second Sunday of Lent, Year B

Psalm 19: Lord, You Have the Words
Third Sunday of Lent, Year B

Ps 19:8, 9, 10, 11

Michael Joncas
Tone 8B: Wisdom Psalm 2

Third Sunday of Lent, Year B

Third Sunday of Lent, Year B

Third Sunday of Lent, Year B

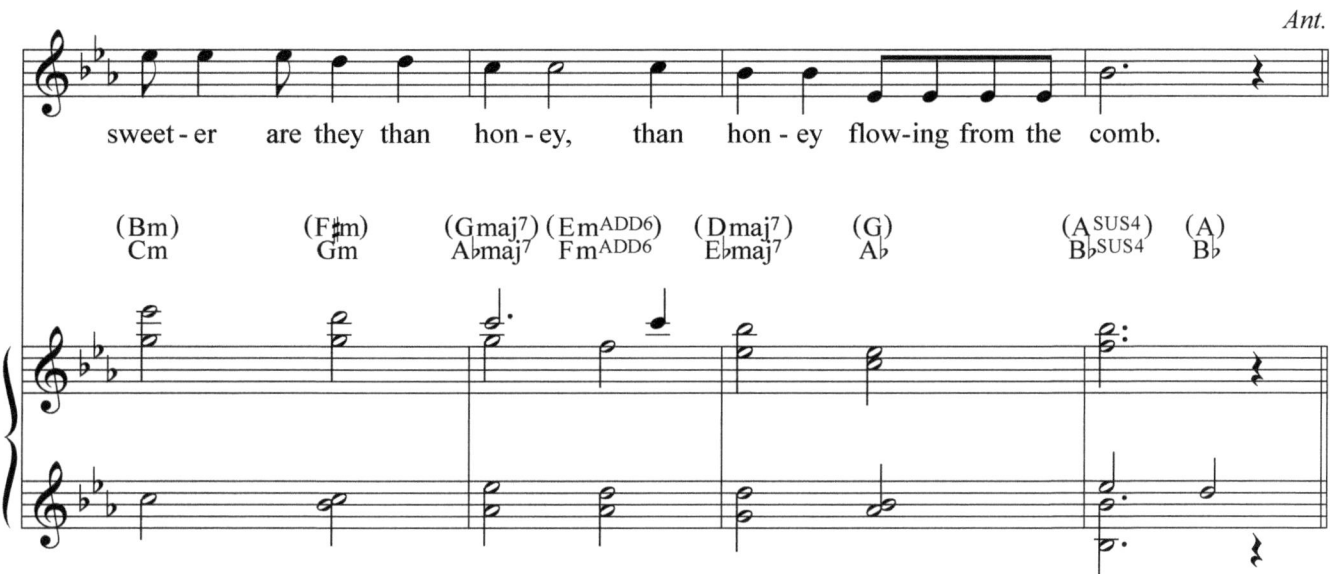

Psalm 137: Let My Tongue Be Silenced
Fourth Sunday of Lent, Year B

Ps 137:1-2, 3, 4-5, 6

Michael Joncas
Tone 4A: Community Lament

Fourth Sunday of Lent, Year B

Fourth Sunday of Lent, Year B

Fourth Sunday of Lent, Year B

Psalm 51: Create a Clean Heart in Me
Fifth Sunday of Lent, Year B

Ps 51:3-4, 12-13, 14-15

Michael Joncas
Tone 4B: Individual Lament

Fifth Sunday of Lent, Year B

Fifth Sunday of Lent, Year B

Fifth Sunday of Lent, Year B

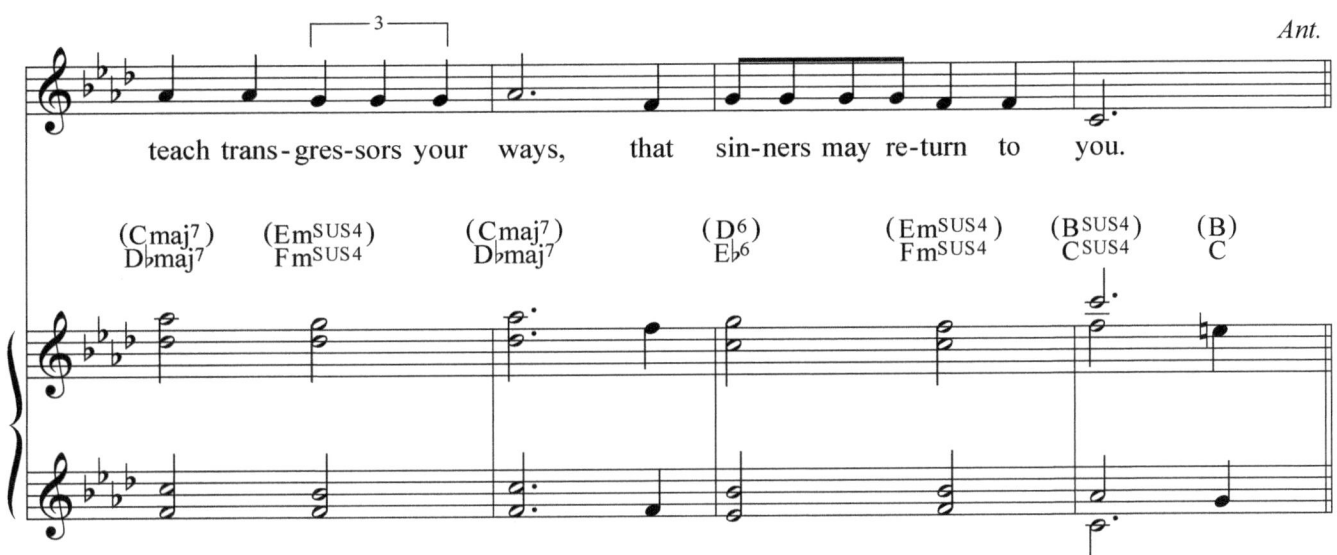

Psalm 118: Give Thanks to the Lord
Second Sunday of Easter/Sunday of Divine Mercy, Years A, B, and C

Ps 118:1-2, 16-17, 22-23

Michael Joncas
Tone 5B: Individual Thanksgiving

Second Sunday of Easter/Sunday of Divine Mercy, Years A, B, and C

Second Sunday of Easter/Sunday of Divine Mercy, Years A, B, and C

Second Sunday of Easter/Sunday of Divine Mercy, Years A, B, and C

Psalm 4: Lord, Let Your Face Shine on Us
Third Sunday of Easter, Year B

Ps 4:2, 4, 7-8, 9

Michael Joncas
Tone 4B: Individual Lament

Third Sunday of Easter, Year B

Third Sunday of Easter, Year B

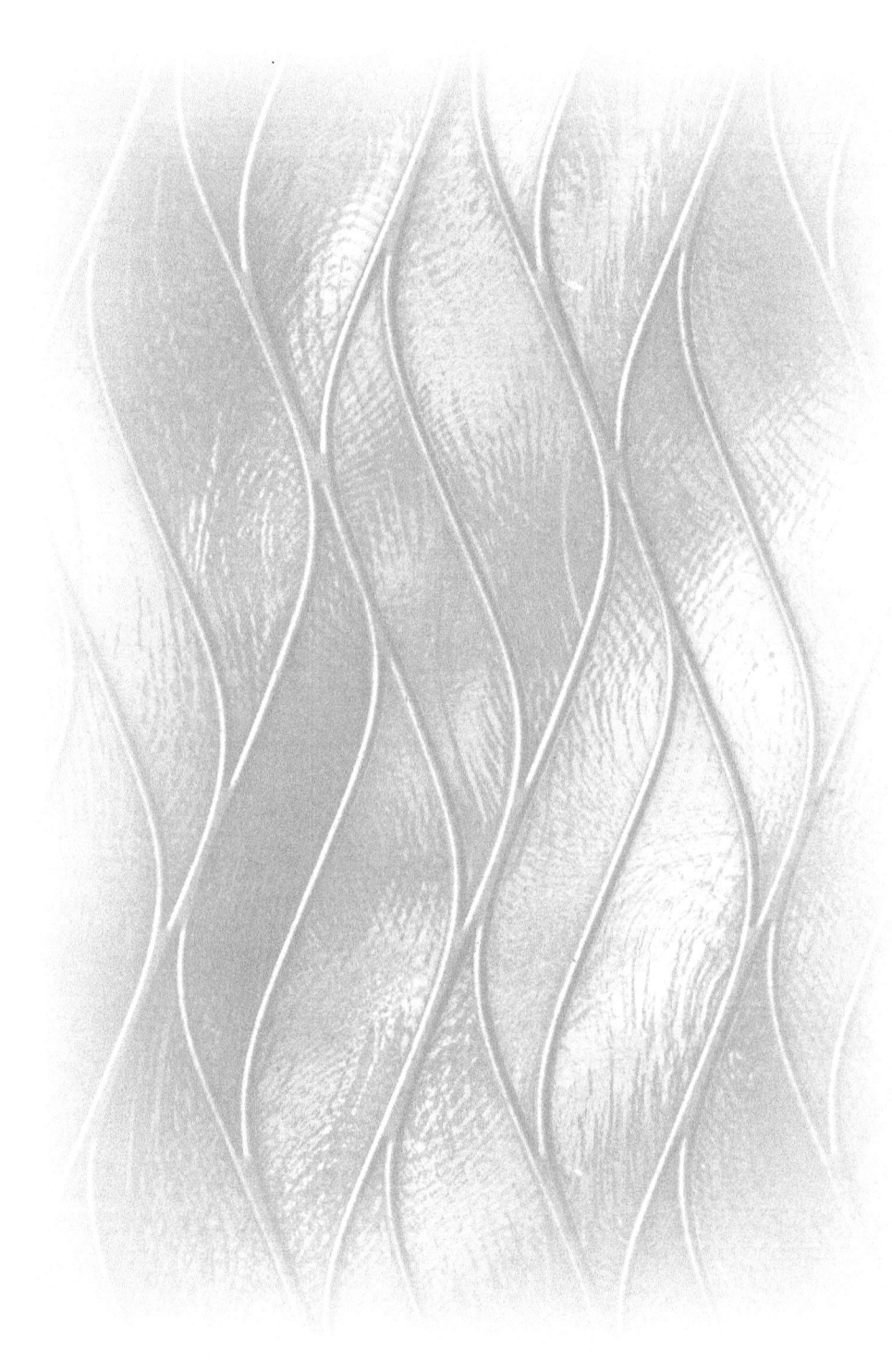

Psalm 118: The Stone Rejected by the Builders
Fourth Sunday of Easter, Year B

Ps 118:1 and 8-9, 21-23, 26 and 28-29

Michael Joncas
Tone 5B: Individual Thanksgiving

Fourth Sunday of Easter, Year B

Fourth Sunday of Easter, Year B

Fourth Sunday of Easter, Year B

Psalm 22: I Will Praise You, Lord
Fifth Sunday of Easter, Year B

Ps 22:26-27, 28, 30, 31-32

Michael Joncas
Tone 5A: Communal Thanksgiving

Fifth Sunday of Easter, Year B

Fifth Sunday of Easter, Year B

Fifth Sunday of Easter, Year B

Fifth Sunday of Easter, Year B

sav - ing   jus - tice   to   peo - ples   yet   un - born:

"These   are   the things   the LORD   has   done."

Psalm 98: The Lord Has Revealed

Sixth Sunday of Easter, Year B

Ps 98:1, 2-3, 3-4

Michael Joncas
Tone 1E: Hymn of Praise to YHWH as King

Text: Refrain, *Lectionary for Mass*, © 1969, 1997, ICEL;
Verses, *The Abbey Psalms and Canticles*, © 2010, 2018, United States Conference of Catholic Bishops, Washington, DC. All rights reserved.
Music: copyright © 2023 The Jan Michael Joncas Trust. Published and administered by Liturgical Press, Collegeville, MN 56321. All rights reserved.

Sixth Sunday of Easter, Year B

Sixth Sunday of Easter, Year B

Psalm 103: The Lord Has Set His Throne

Seventh Sunday of Easter, Year B

Ps 103:1-2, 11-12, 19-20

Michael Joncas
Tone 5B: Individual Thanksgiving

Antiphon
Simply ♩ = 80

Harmony / Melody:
The Lord has set, set his throne in heav - en.
The Lord has set his throne, set his throne in heav - en.

D Bm G F♯ Bm E⁷ G A D

Alternate Antiphon

Al - le - lu - ia, al - le - lu - ia, al - le - lu - ia.
Al - le - lu - ia, al - le - lu - ia, al - le - lu - ia.

D Bm G F♯ Bm E⁷ G A D

Seventh Sunday of Easter, Year B

Seventh Sunday of Easter, Year B

Psalm 33: Blessed the People
Solemnity of the Most Holy Trinity, Year B

Ps 33:4-5, 6, 9, 18-19, 20, 22

Michael Joncas
Tone 1B: Hymn of Praise,
Motivation from History or Torah

Solemnity of the Most Holy Trinity, Year B

Solemnity of the Most Holy Trinity, Year B

Solemnity of the Most Holy Trinity, Year B

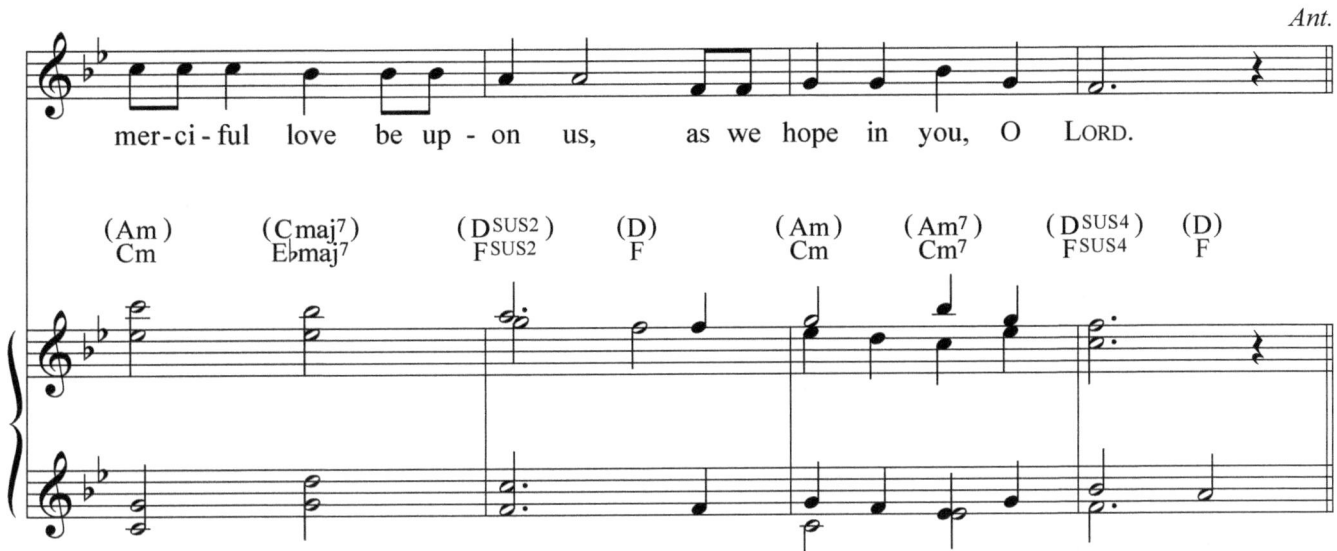

Psalm 116: I Will Take the Cup of Salvation
Solemnity of the Body and Blood of Christ, Year B

Ps 116:12-13, 15-16, 17-18

Michael Joncas
Tone 5B: Individual Thanksgiving

Solemnity of the Body and Blood of Christ, Year B

Verse 1

1. How can I re-pay the LORD for all his good-ness to me? The cup of sal-va-tion I will raise; I will call on the name of the LORD.

Ant.

Verse 2

2. How pre-cious in the eyes of the LORD is the death of his faith-ful. Your

Solemnity of the Body and Blood of Christ, Year B

Ant.

vows   to   the LORD I   will ful - fill   be - fore   all   his   peo - ple.

Psalm 40: Here Am I, Lord
Second Sunday in Ordinary Time, Year B

Ps 40:2, 4, 7-8, 8-9, 10

Michael Joncas
Tone 5B: Individual Thanksgiving

Second Sunday in Ordinary Time, Year B

Second Sunday in Ordinary Time, Year B

Second Sunday in Ordinary Time, Year B

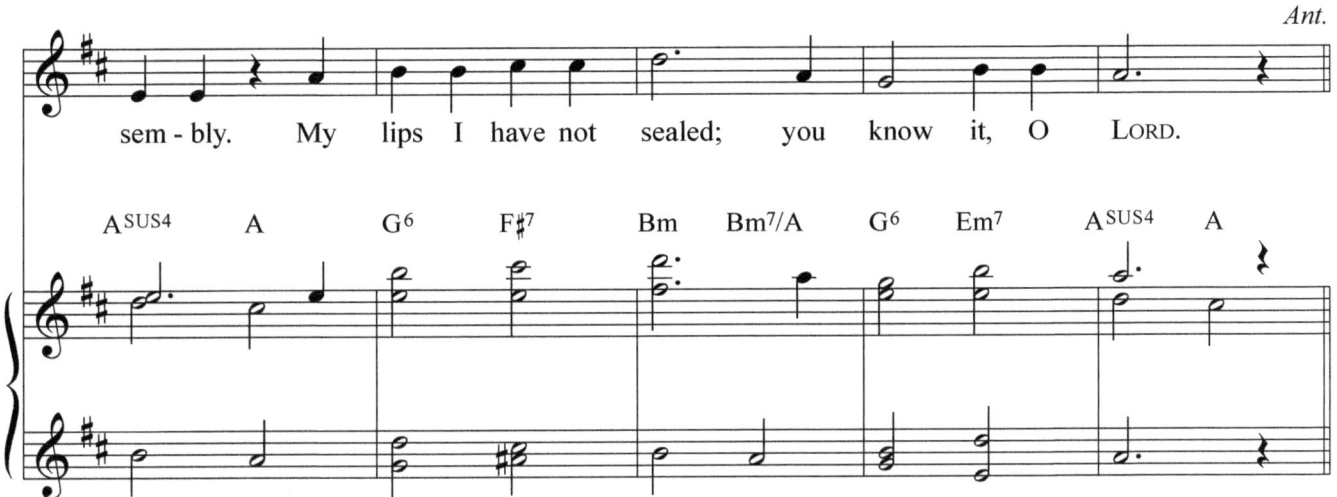

Psalm 25: Teach Me Your Ways

Third Sunday in Ordinary Time, Year B

Ps 25:4-5, 6, 7, 8-9

Michael Joncas
Tone 8B: Wisdom Psalm 2

Third Sunday in Ordinary Time, Year B

Third Sunday in Ordinary Time, Year B

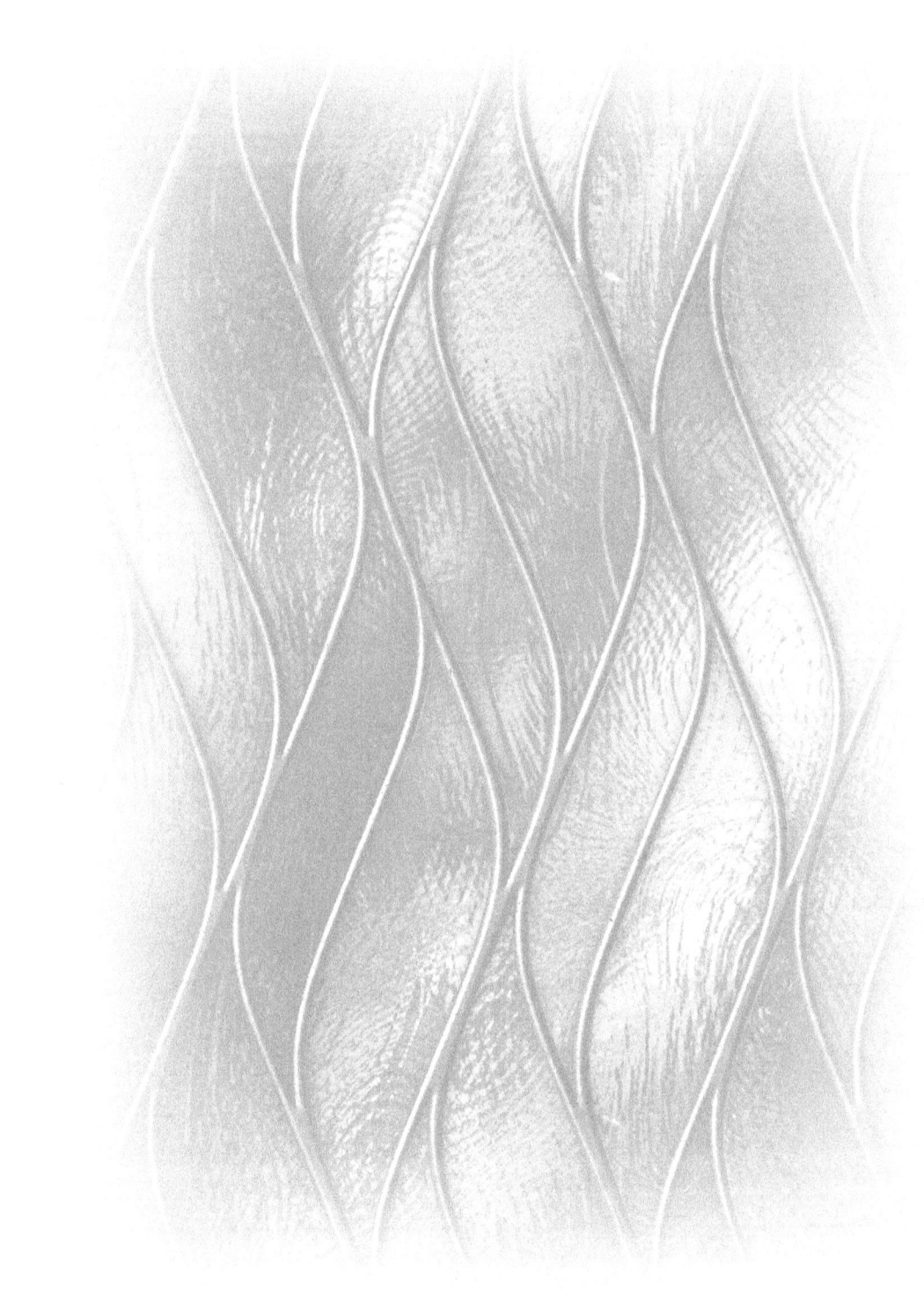

Psalm 95: If Today You Hear His Voice

Fourth Sunday in Ordinary Time, Year B

Ps 95:1-2, 6-7, 7-9

Michael Joncas
Tone 1D: Processional

Fourth Sunday in Ordinary Time, Year B

Fourth Sunday in Ordinary Time, Year B

Fourth Sunday in Ordinary Time, Year B

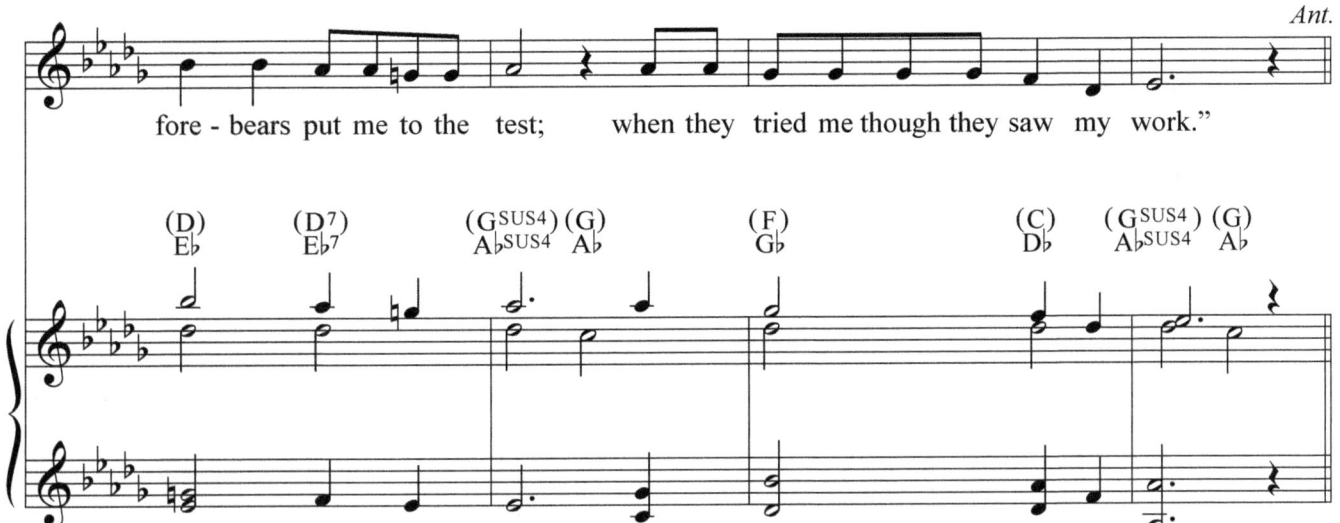

fore - bears put me to the test;   when they tried me though they saw my work."

Psalm 147: Praise the Lord Who Heals

Fifth Sunday in Ordinary Time, Year B

Ps 147:1-2, 3-4, 5-6

Michael Joncas
Tone 1B: Hymn of Praise,
Motivation from History or Torah

Fifth Sunday in Ordinary Time, Year B

Fifth Sunday in Ordinary Time, Year B

Psalm 32: I Turn to You, Lord
Sixth Sunday in Ordinary Time, Year B

Ps 32:1-2, 5, 11

Michael Joncas
Tone 8A: Wisdom Psalm 1

Sixth Sunday in Ordinary Time, Year B

Sixth Sunday in Ordinary Time, Year B

Psalm 41: Lord, Heal My Soul
Seventh Sunday in Ordinary Time, Year B

Ps 41:2-3, 4-5, 13-14

Michael Joncas
Tone 6: Psalm of Confidence

Seventh Sunday in Ordinary Time, Year B

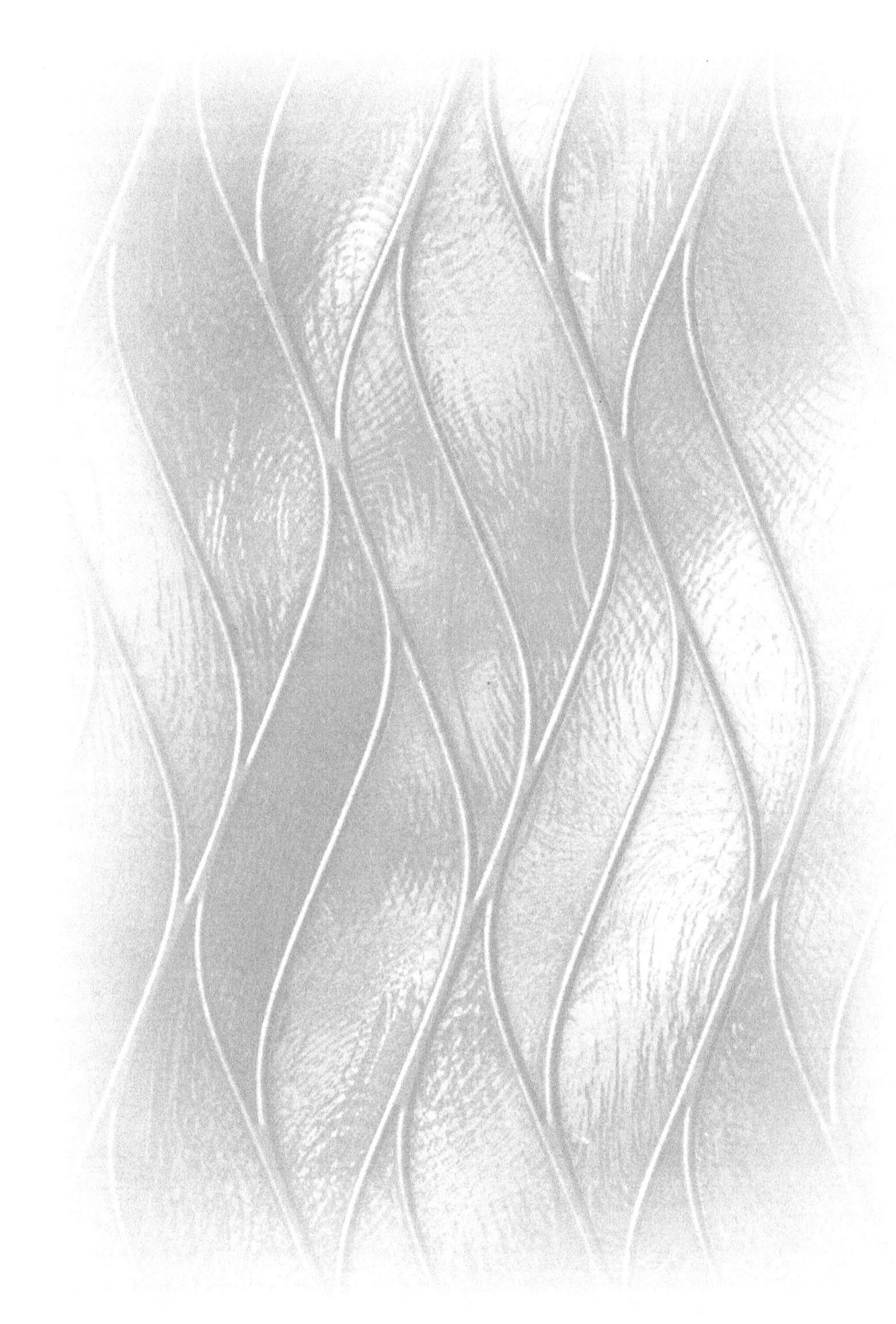

Psalm 103: The Lord Is Kind
Eighth Sunday in Ordinary Time, Year B

Ps 103:1-2, 3-4, 8, 10, 12-13

Michael Joncas
Tone 5B: Individual Thanksgiving

Eighth Sunday in Ordinary Time, Year B

Eighth Sunday in Ordinary Time, Year B

Eighth Sunday in Ordinary Time, Year B

Psalm 81: Sing with Joy
Ninth Sunday in Ordinary Time, Year B

Ps 81:3-4, 5-6, 6-8, 10-11

Michael Joncas
Tone 3: Prophetic Psalm

Ninth Sunday in Ordinary Time, Year B

Ninth Sunday in Ordinary Time, Year B

Ninth Sunday in Ordinary Time, Year B

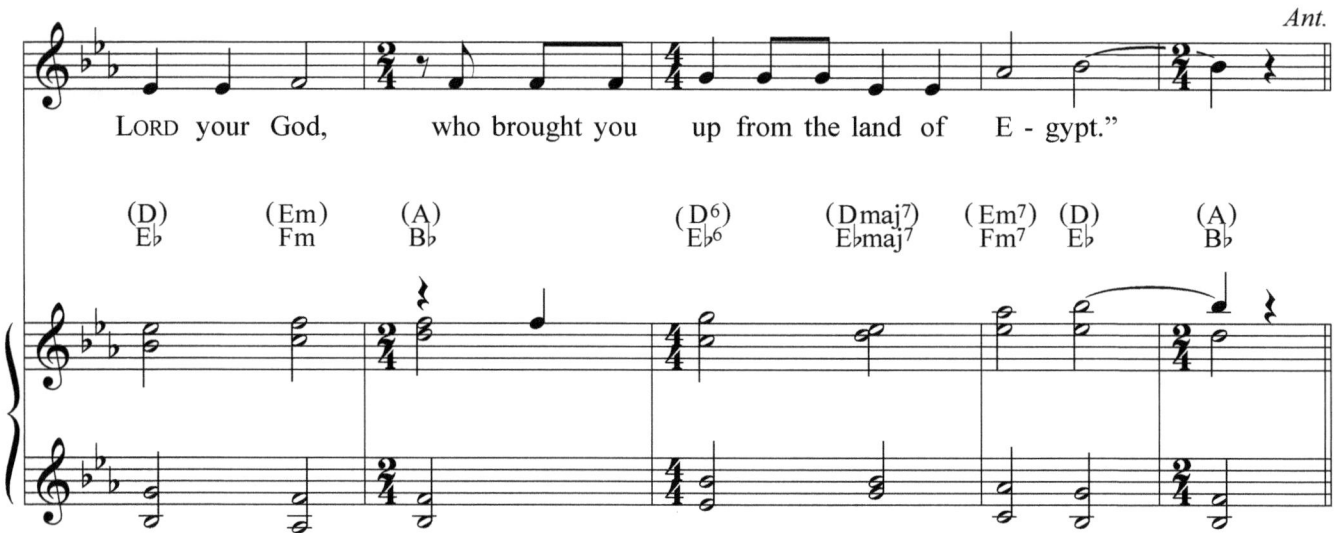

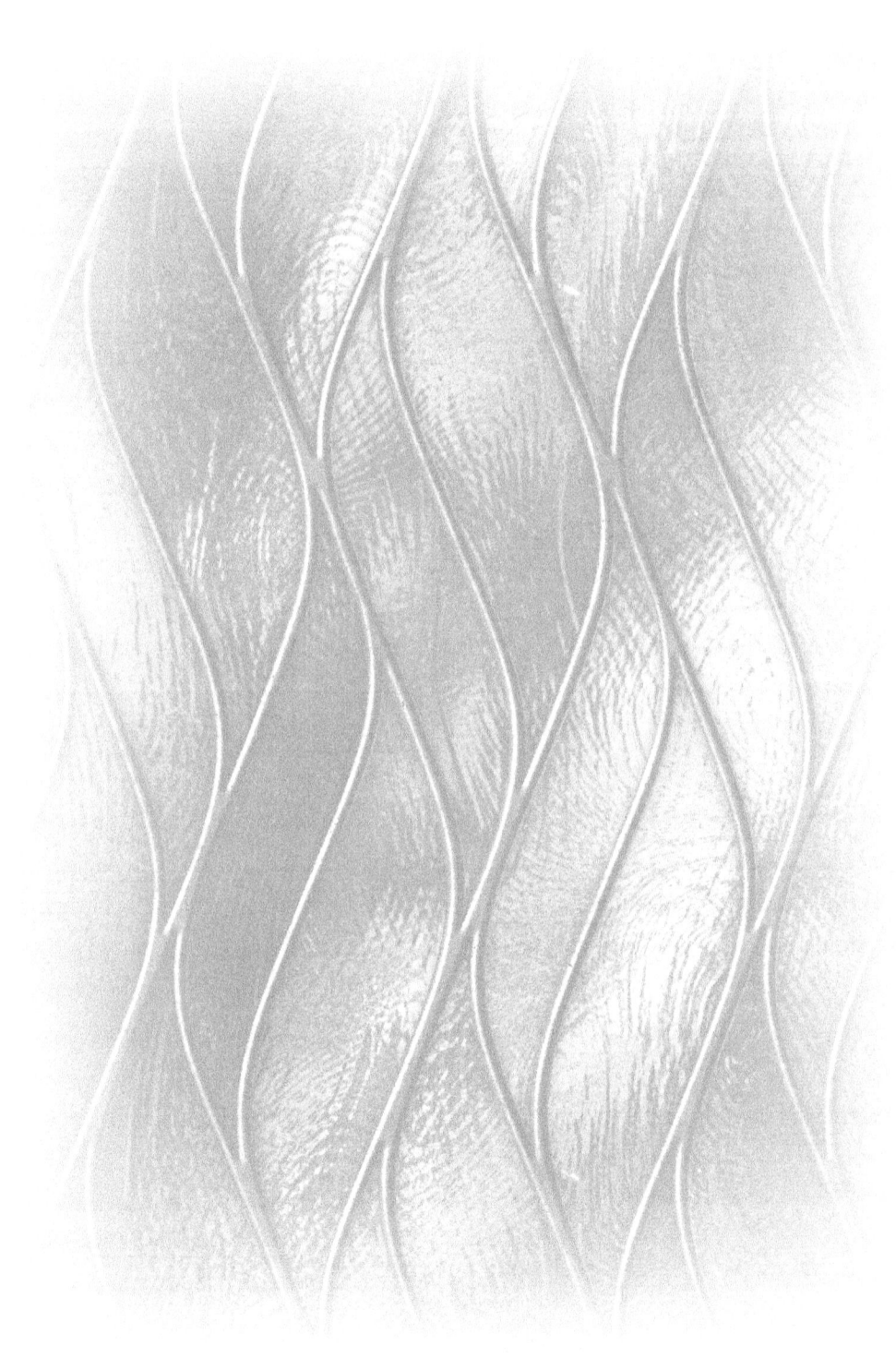

Psalm 130: With the Lord There Is Mercy
Tenth Sunday in Ordinary Time, Year B

Ps 130:1-2, 3-4, 5-6, 7-8

Michael Joncas
Tone 4B: Individual Lament

With the Lord there is mer - cy and full-ness of re-demp-tion.

With the Lord there is mer - cy and full-ness of re-demp-tion.

Verse 1

1. Out of the depths I cry to you, O Lord; Lord, hear my voice! O

Tenth Sunday in Ordinary Time, Year B

Tenth Sunday in Ordinary Time, Year B

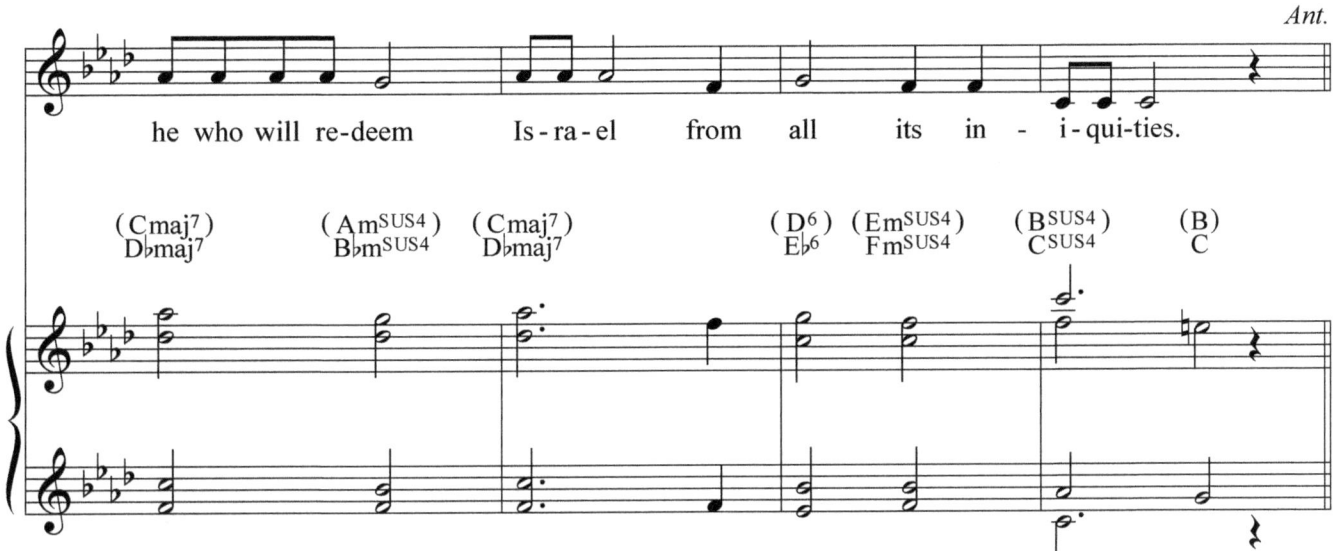

Psalm 92: Lord, It Is Good
Eleventh Sunday in Ordinary Time, Year B

Ps 92:2-3, 13-14, 15-16

Michael Joncas
Tone 5A: Communal Thanksgiving

Antiphon

Proclamatory ♩ = 80

Harmony

Lord, it is good to give thanks to you, to give thanks to you.

Melody

Lord, it is good to give thanks to you, to give thanks to you.

Verse 1

1. It is good to give thanks to the LORD, to make mu-sic to your name, O

Eleventh Sunday in Ordinary Time, Year B

Eleventh Sunday in Ordinary Time, Year B

Eleventh Sunday in Ordinary Time, Year B

Psalm 107: Give Thanks to the Lord
Twelfth Sunday in Ordinary Time, Year B

Ps 107:23-24, 25-26, 28-29, 30-31

Michael Joncas
Tone 1B: Hymn of Praise,
Motivation from History or Torah

Twelfth Sunday in Ordinary Time, Year B

Twelfth Sunday in Ordinary Time, Year B

Twelfth Sunday in Ordinary Time, Year B

Psalm 30: I Will Praise You, Lord
Thirteenth Sunday in Ordinary Time, Year B

Ps 30:2, 4, 5-6, 11-12, 13

Michael Joncas
Tone 4C: Prayer for the Sick

Thirteenth Sunday in Ordinary Time, Year B

Thirteenth Sunday in Ordinary Time, Year B

Psalm 123: Our Eyes Are Fixed on the Lord

Fourteenth Sunday in Ordinary Time, Year B

Ps 123:1-2, 2, 3-4

Michael Joncas
Tone 4B: Individual Lament

Antiphon

Pleading ♩ = 85

Harmony: Our eyes are fixed, plead-ing for his mer-cy.

Melody: Our eyes are fixed on the Lord, plead-ing for his mer-cy.

Verse 1

1. To you have I lift-ed up my eyes, you who dwell in the

Fourteenth Sunday in Ordinary Time, Year B

Fourteenth Sunday in Ordinary Time, Year B

Psalm 85: Lord, Let Us See Your Kindness
Fifteenth Sunday in Ordinary Time, Year B

Ps 85:9-10, 11-12, 13-14

Michael Joncas
Tone 3: Prophetic Psalm

Fifteenth Sunday in Ordinary Time, Year B

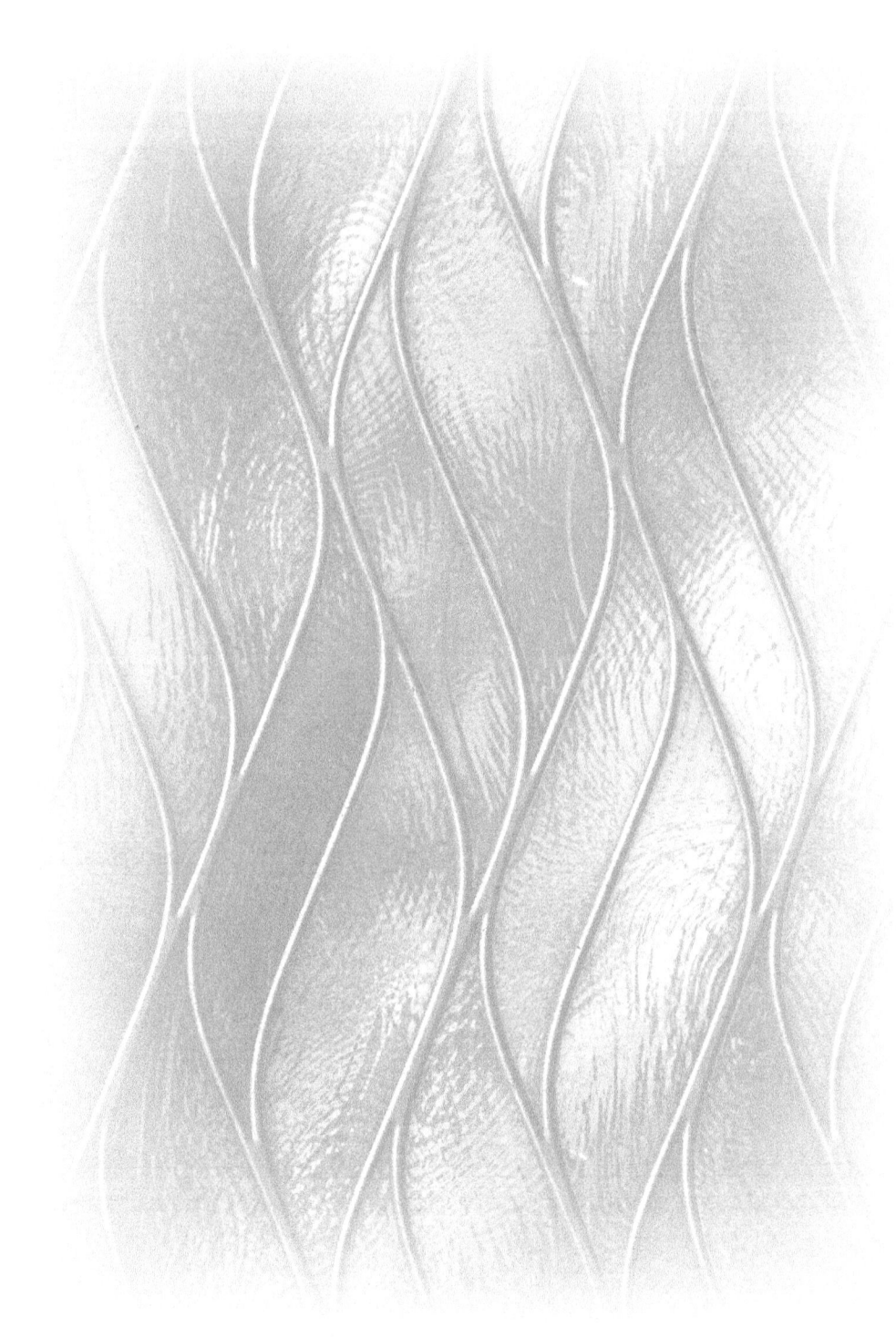

Psalm 23: The Lord Is My Shepherd
Sixteenth Sunday in Ordinary Time, Year B

Ps 23:1-3, 3-4, 5, 6

Michael Joncas
Tone 6: Psalm of Confidence

Sixteenth Sunday in Ordinary Time, Year B

Sixteenth Sunday in Ordinary Time, Year B

Psalm 145: The Hand of the Lord
Seventeenth Sunday in Ordinary Time, Year B

Ps 145:10-11, 15-16, 17-18

Michael Joncas
Tone 1B: Hymn of Praise,
Motivation from History or Torah

Seventeenth Sunday in Ordinary Time, Year B

Seventeenth Sunday in Ordinary Time, Year B

Psalm 78: The Lord Gave Them Bread

Eighteenth Sunday in Ordinary Time, Year B

Ps 78:3-4, 23-24, 25, 54

Michael Joncas
Tone 1B: Hymn of Praise,
Motivation from history or Torah

Eighteenth Sunday in Ordinary Time, Year B

Psalm 34: Taste and See
Nineteenth Sunday in Ordinary Time, Year B

Ps 34:2-3, 4-5, 6-7, 8-9

Michael Joncas
Tone 8A: Wisdom Psalm 1

Nineteenth Sunday in Ordinary Time, Year B

Nineteenth Sunday in Ordinary Time, Year B

Nineteenth Sunday in Ordinary Time, Year B

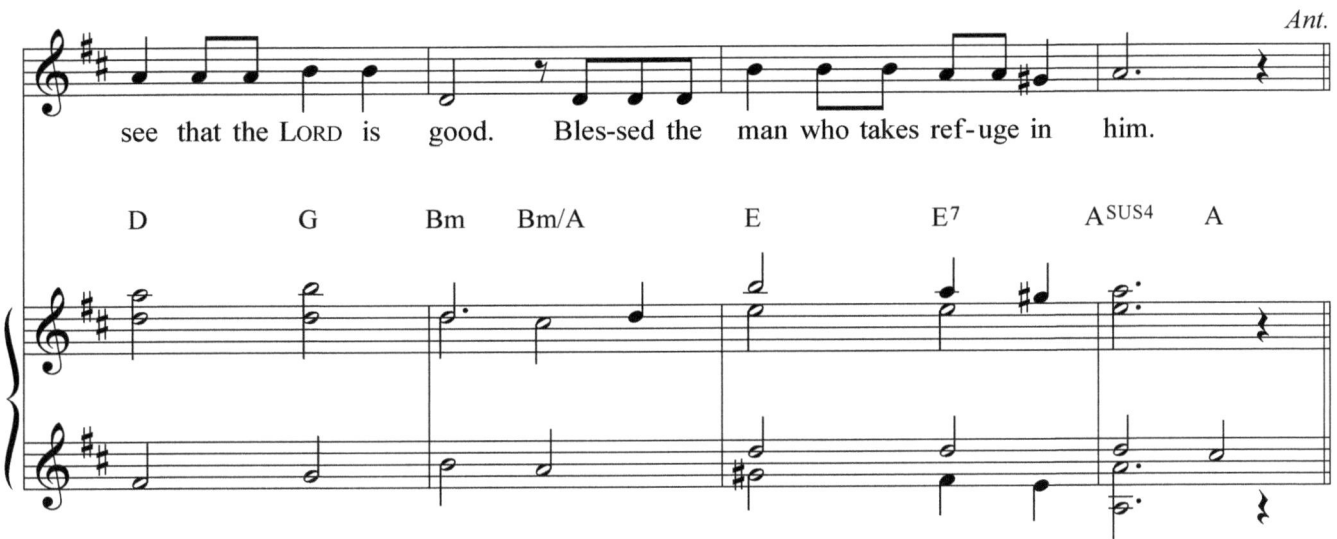

140

Psalm 34: Taste and See
Twentieth Sunday in Ordinary Time, Year B

Ps 34:2-3, 4-5, 6-7

Michael Joncas
Tone 8A: Wisdom Psalm 1

Twentieth Sunday in Ordinary Time, Year B

Twentieth Sunday in Ordinary Time, Year B

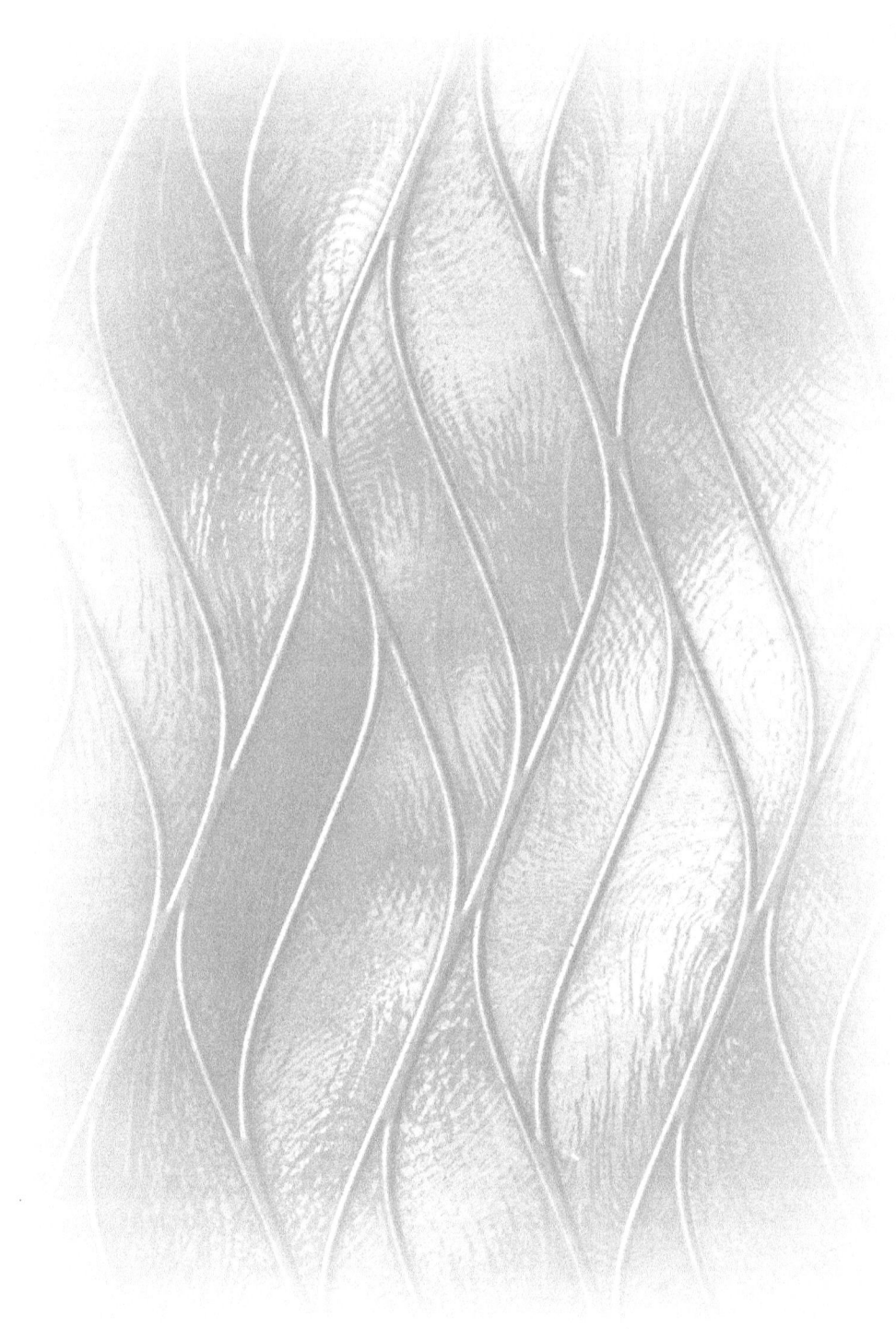

Psalm 34: Taste and See
Twenty-First Sunday in Ordinary Time, Year B

Ps 34:2-3, 16-17, 18-19, 20-21

Michael Joncas
Tone 8A: Wisdom Psalm 1

Antiphon
With delight ♩ = 80

Taste and see the good-ness of the Lord.

Taste and see the good - ness of the Lord.

Verse 1

1. I will bless the LORD at all times, praise of him is al-ways in my mouth. In the

Twenty-First Sunday in Ordinary Time, Year B

Twenty-First Sunday in Ordinary Time, Year B

Twenty-First Sunday in Ordinary Time, Year B

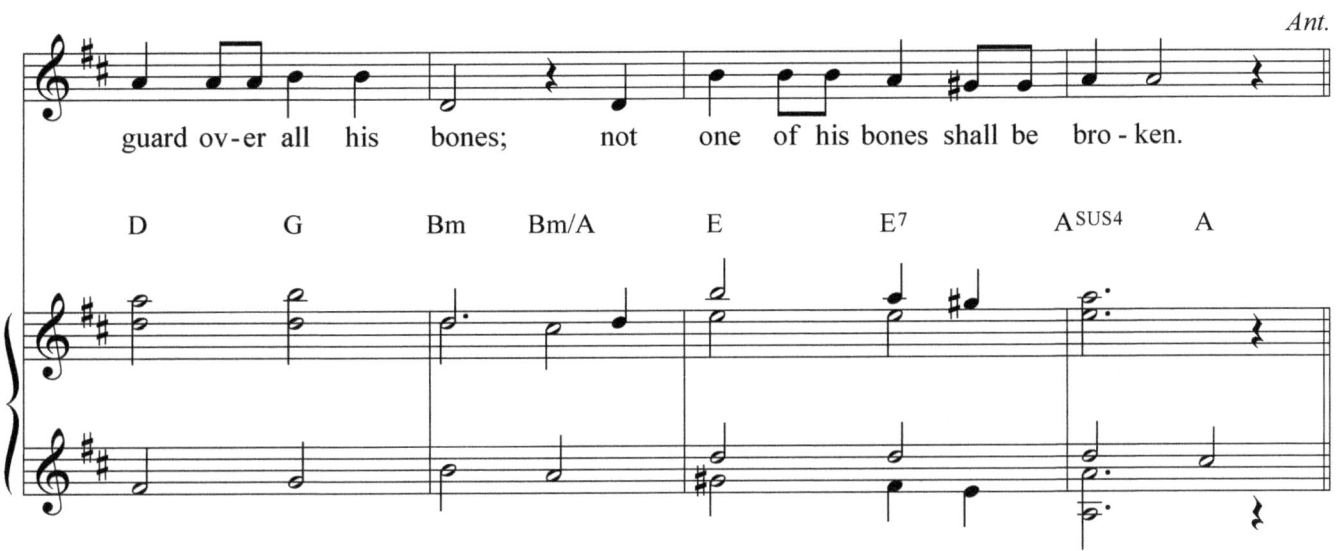

Psalm 15: One Who Does Justice
Twenty-Second Sunday in Ordinary Time, Year B

Ps 15:2-3, 3-4, 5

Michael Joncas
Tone 1D: Processional

Antiphon

With confidence ♩ = 90

The one who does jus-tice will live in the pres-ence of the Lord.

The one who does jus-tice will live in the pres-ence of the Lord.

Verse 1

1. Who-ev-er walks with-out fault, who does what is up-right, and

Twenty-Second Sunday in Ordinary Time, Year B

Twenty-Second Sunday in Ordinary Time, Year B

Verse 3

3. Who lends no mon-ey at in - t'rest, and ac - cepts no bribe a-gainst the

Cmaj⁷ F C G^SUS4 G F G

in - no-cent. Such a one shall nev - er be sha - ken.

Ant.

C^SUS4 C F C G^SUS4 G

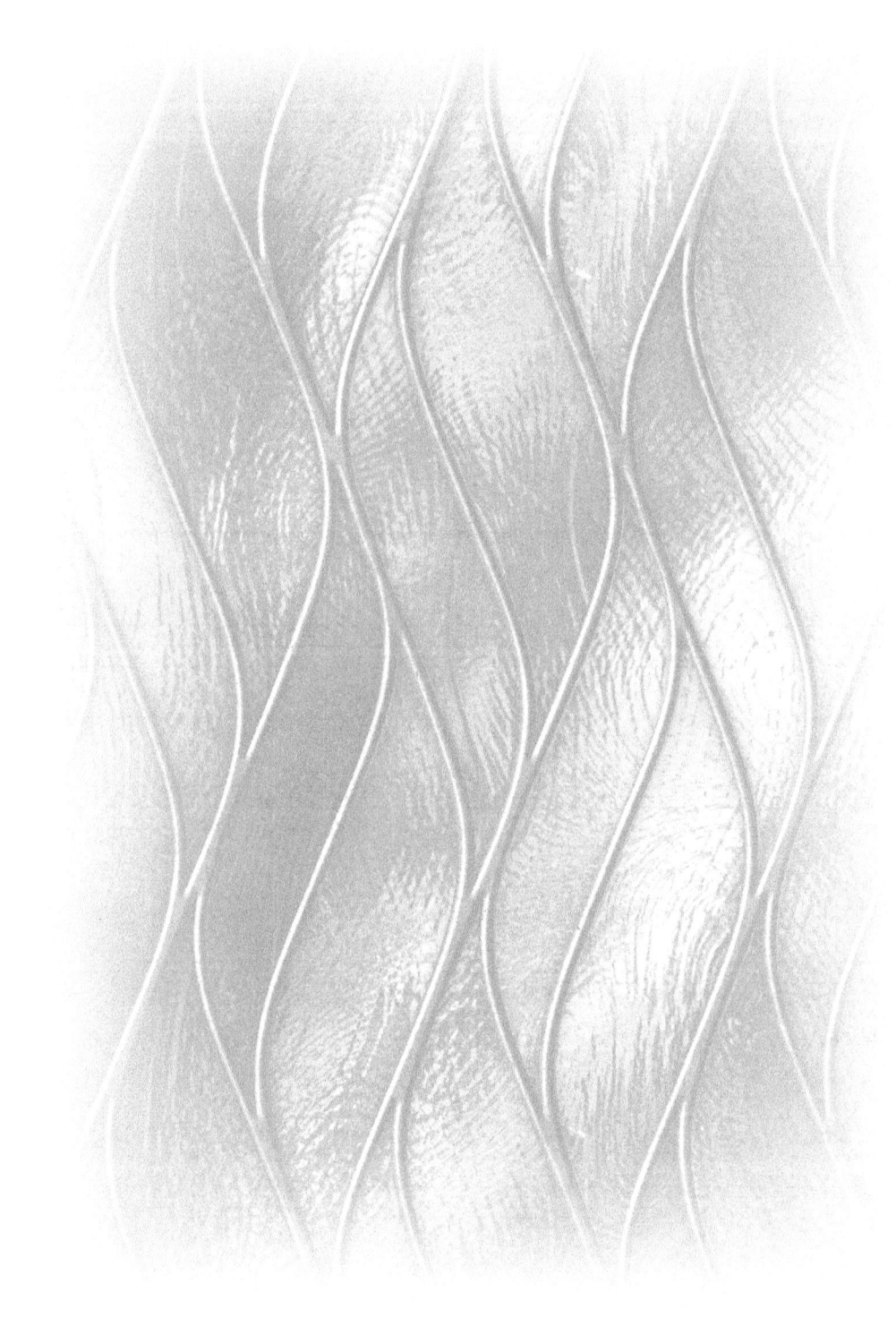

Psalm 146: Praise the Lord, My Soul
Twenty-Third Sunday in Ordinary Time, Year B

Ps 146:6-7, 8-9, 9-10

Michael Joncas
Tone 1B: Hymn of Praise,
Motivation from History or Torah

Twenty-Third Sunday in Ordinary Time, Year B

Twenty-Third Sunday in Ordinary Time, Year B

Twenty-Third Sunday in Ordinary Time, Year B

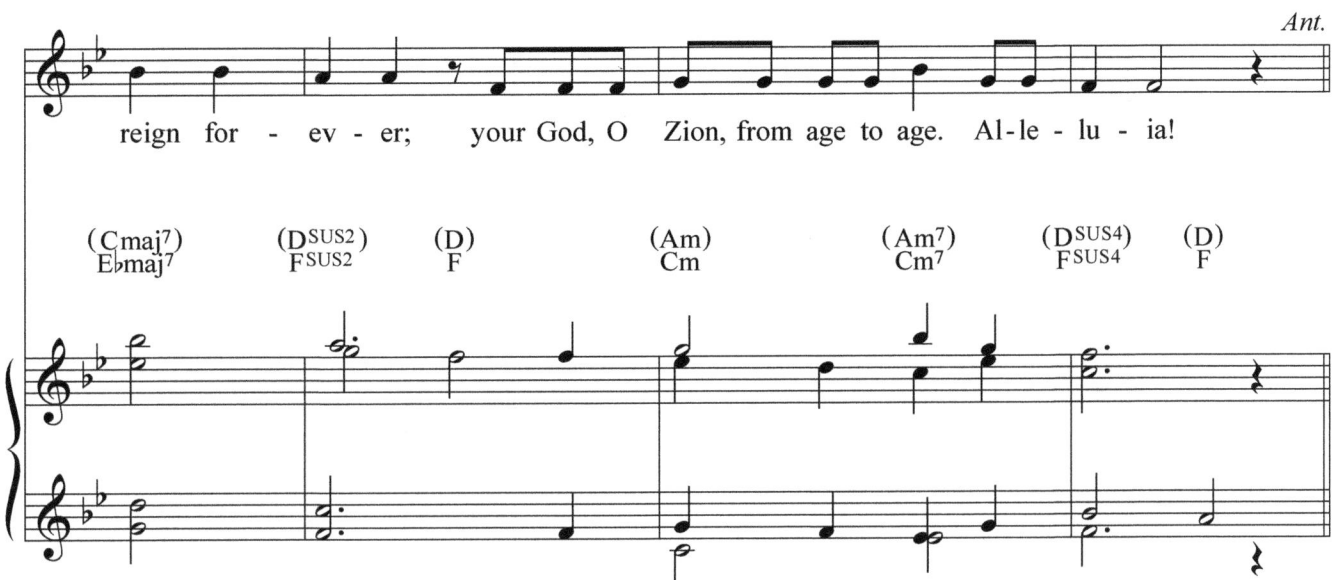

Psalm 116: I Will Walk before the Lord
Twenty-Fourth Sunday in Ordinary Time, Year B

Ps 116:1-2, 3-4, 5-6, 8-9

Michael Joncas
Tone 5B: Individual Thanksgiving

Twenty-Fourth Sunday in Ordinary Time, Year B

Twenty-Fourth Sunday in Ordinary Time, Year B

Psalm 54: The Lord Upholds My Life
Twenty-Fifth Sunday in Ordinary Time, Year B

Ps 54:3-4, 5, 6 and 8

Michael Joncas
Tone 4B: Individual Lament

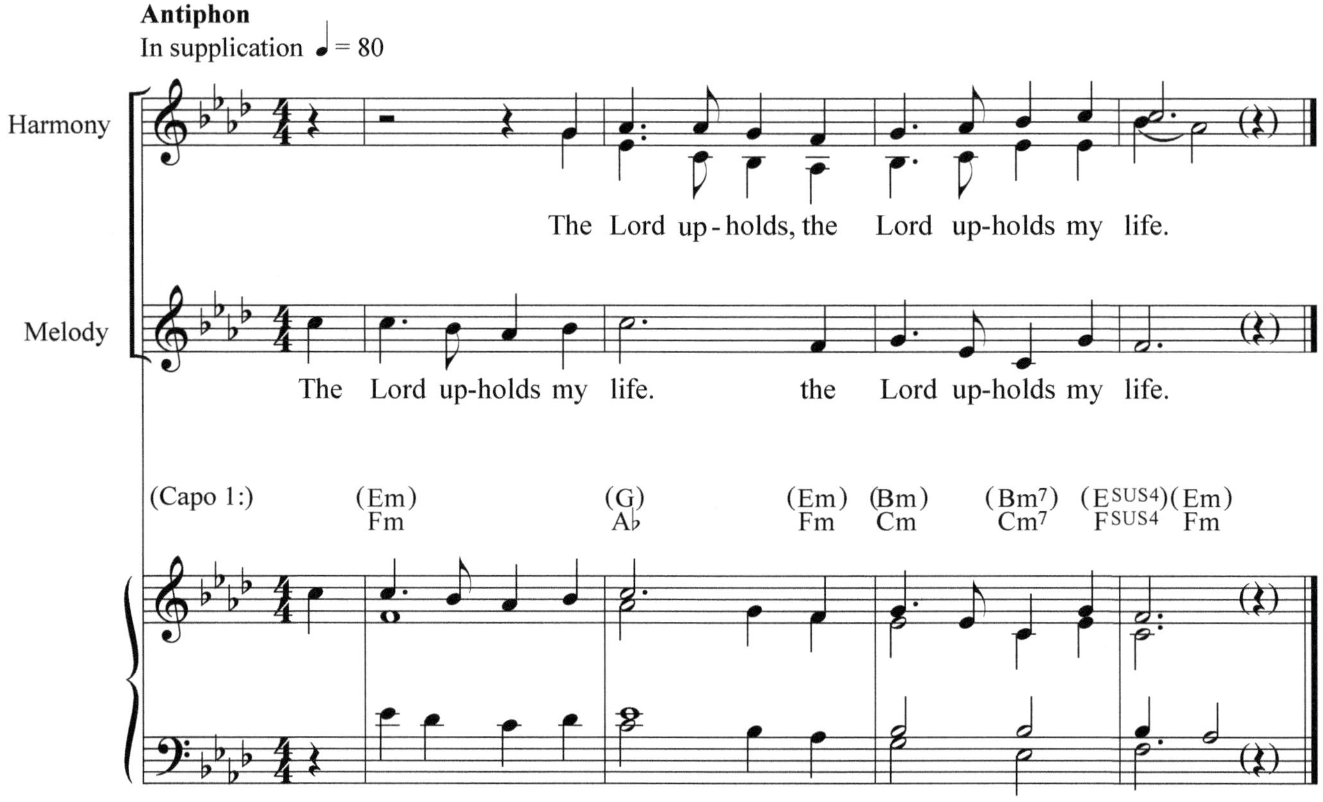

Twenty-Fifth Sunday in Ordinary Time, Year B

Twenty-Fifth Sunday in Ordinary Time, Year B

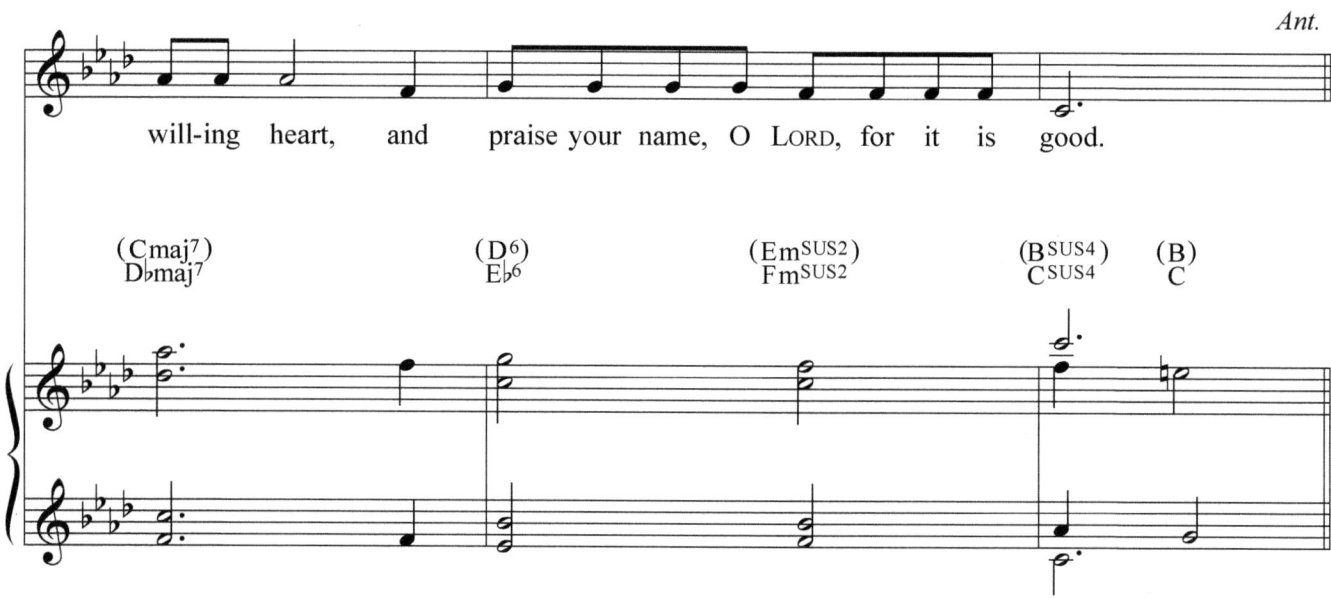

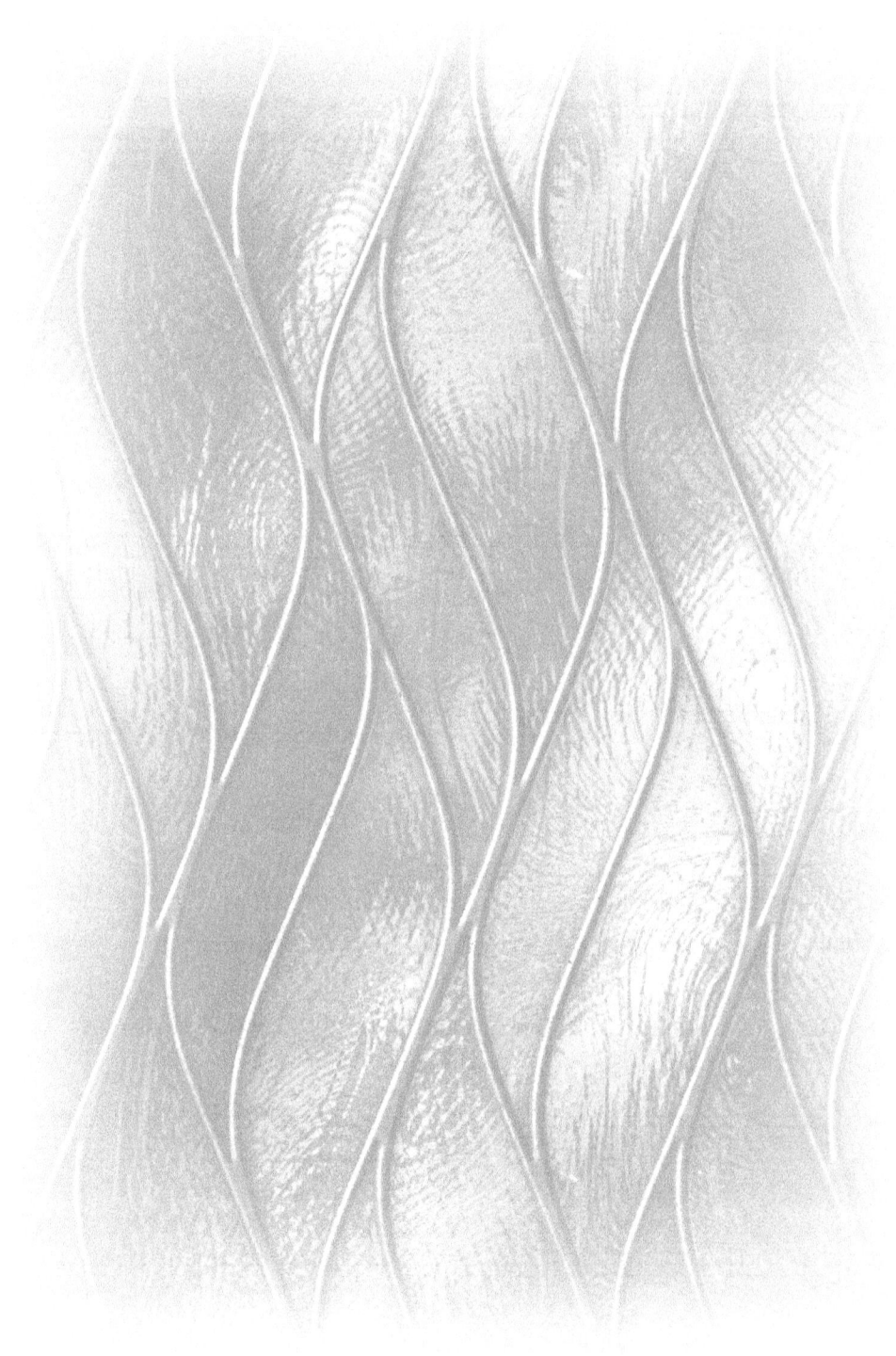

Psalm 19: The Precepts of the Lord
Twenty-Sixth Sunday in Ordinary Time, Year B

Ps 19:8, 10, 12, 13-14

Michael Joncas
Tone 8B: Wisdom Psalm 2

Antiphon

Simply ♩ = 80

The pre - cepts of the Lord give joy to the heart.

The pre - cepts of the Lord give joy to the heart.

Verse 1

1. The law of the LORD is per - fect; it re - vives the soul. The de -

Twenty-Sixth Sunday in Ordinary Time, Year B

Twenty-Sixth Sunday in Ordinary Time, Year B

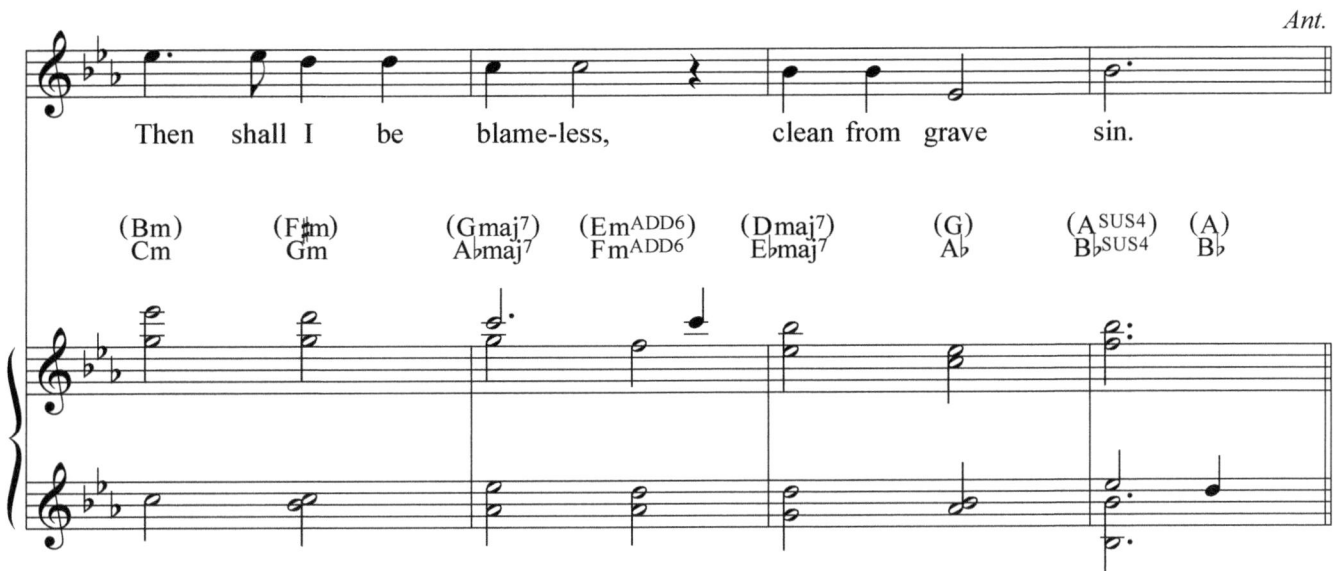

Psalm 128: May the Lord Bless Us
Twenty-Seventh Sunday in Ordinary Time, Year B

Ps 128:1-2, 3, 4-5, 6

Michael Joncas
Tone 8B: Wisdom Psalm 2

Twenty-Seventh Sunday in Ordinary Time, Year B

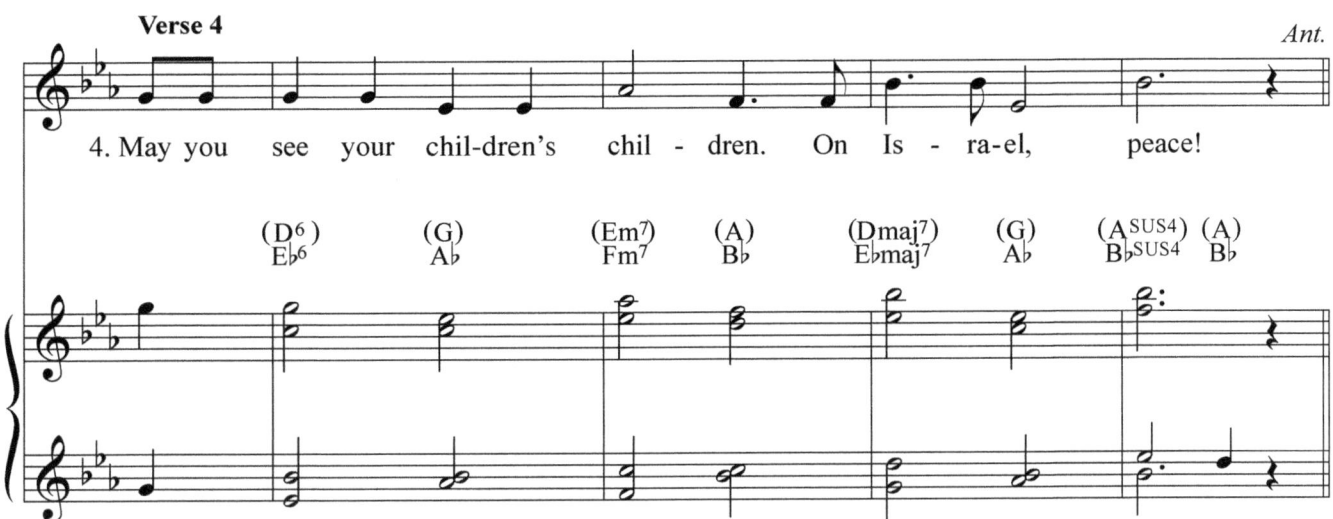

Psalm 90: Fill Us with Your Love
Twenty-Eighth Sunday in Ordinary Time, Year B

Ps 90:12-13, 14-15, 16-17

Michael Joncas
Tone 4A: Community Lament

Twenty-Eighth Sunday in Ordinary Time, Year B

Twenty-Eighth Sunday in Ordinary Time, Year B

Psalm 33: Lord, Let Your Mercy

Twenty-Ninth Sunday in Ordinary Time, Year B

Ps 33:4-5, 18-19, 20, 22

Michael Joncas
Tone 1B: Hymn of Praise,
Motivation from History or Torah

Twenty-Ninth Sunday in Ordinary Time, Year B

Twenty-Ninth Sunday in Ordinary Time, Year B

Psalm 126: The Lord Has Done Great Things
Thirtieth Sunday in Ordinary Time, Year B

Ps 126:1-2, 2-3, 4-5, 6

Michael Joncas
Tone 1B: Hymn of Praise,
Motivation from History or Torah

Thirtieth Sunday in Ordinary Time, Year B

Thirtieth Sunday in Ordinary Time, Year B

Thirtieth Sunday in Ordinary Time, Year B

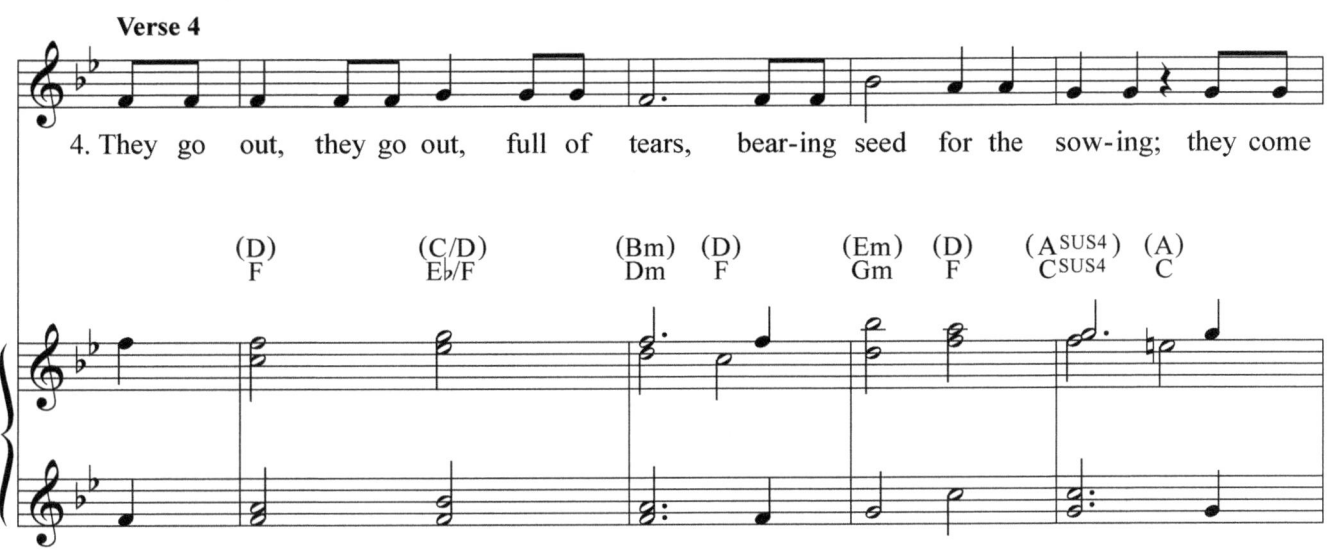

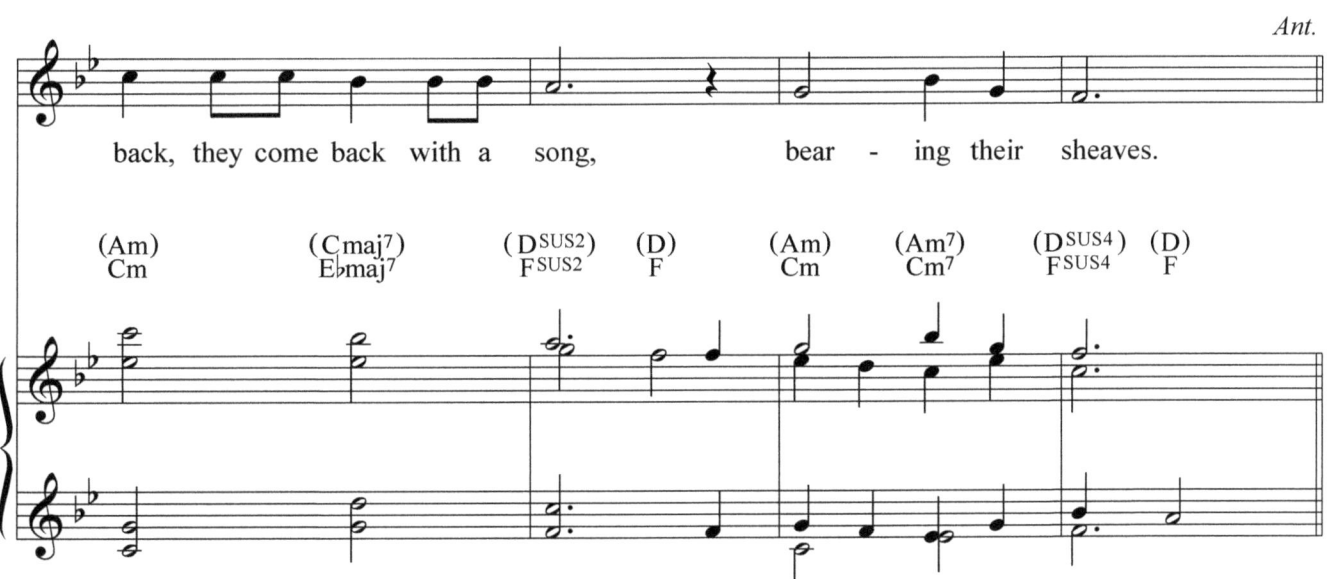

Psalm 18: I Love You Lord, My Strength
Thirty-First Sunday in Ordinary Time, Year B

Ps 18:2-3, 3-4, 47, 51

Michael Joncas
Tone 2C: Royal Song of Thanksgiving

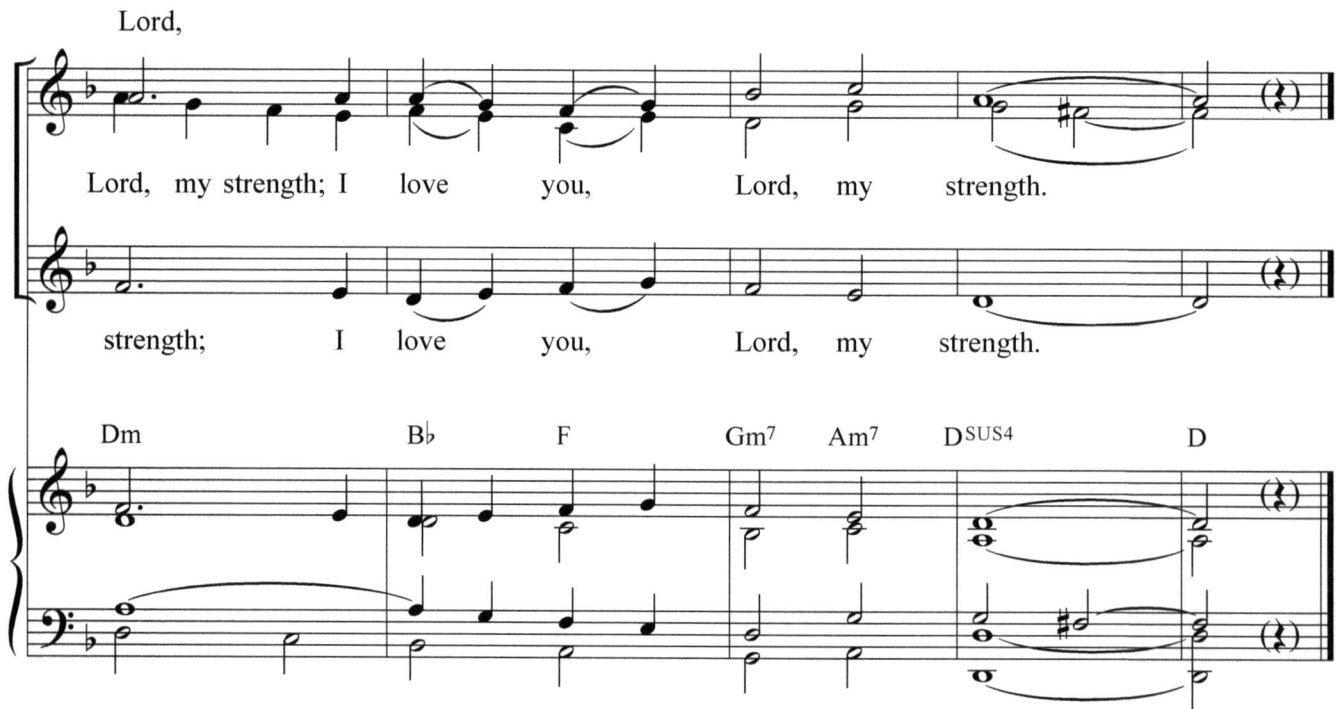

Thirty-First Sunday in Ordinary Time, Year B

Thirty-First Sunday in Ordinary Time, Year B

Thirty-First Sunday in Ordinary Time, Year B

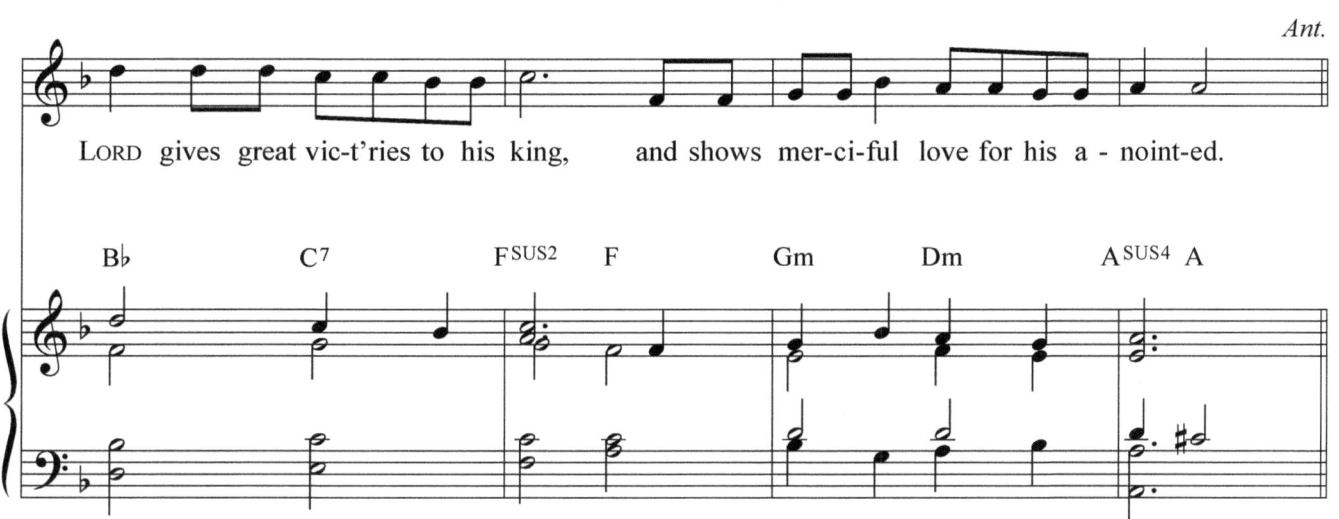

Psalm 146: Praise the Lord, My Soul
Thirty-Second Sunday in Ordinary Time, Year B

Ps 146:6-7, 8-9, 9-10

Michael Joncas
Tone 1B: Hymn of Praise,
Motivation from History or Torah

Thirty-Second Sunday in Ordinary Time, Year B

Thirty-Second Sunday in Ordinary Time, Year B

Thirty-Second Sunday in Ordinary Time, Year B

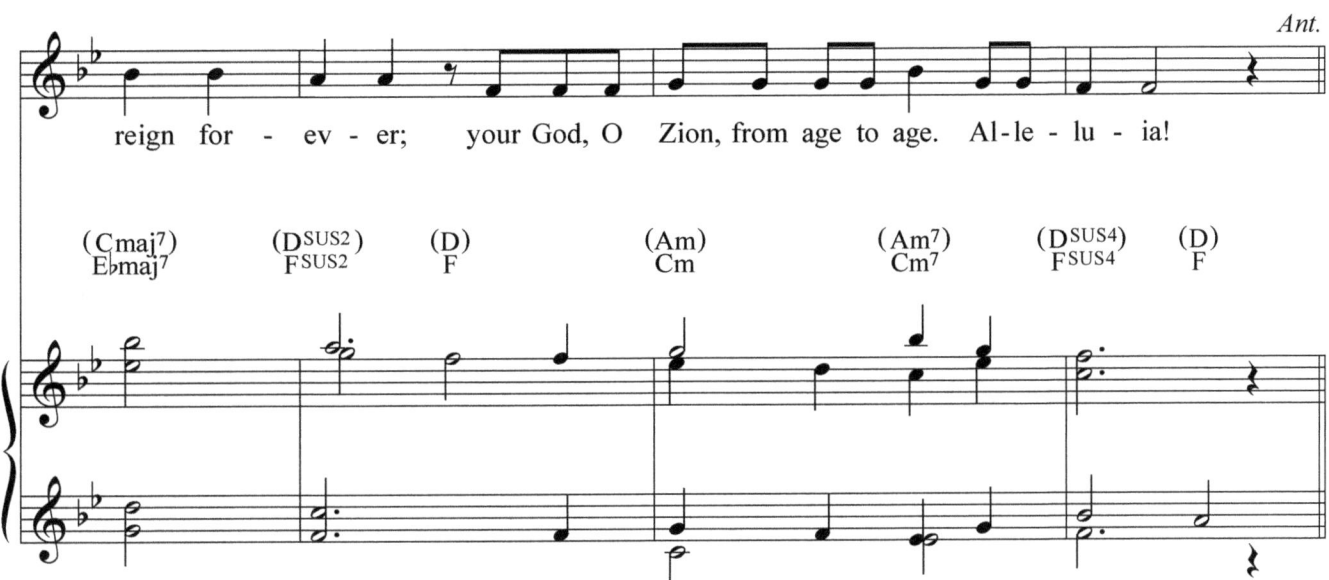

Psalm 16: You Are My Inheritance
Thirty-Third Sunday in Ordinary Time, Year B

Ps 16:5, 8, 9-10, 11

Michael Joncas
Tone 4C: Prayer for the Sick

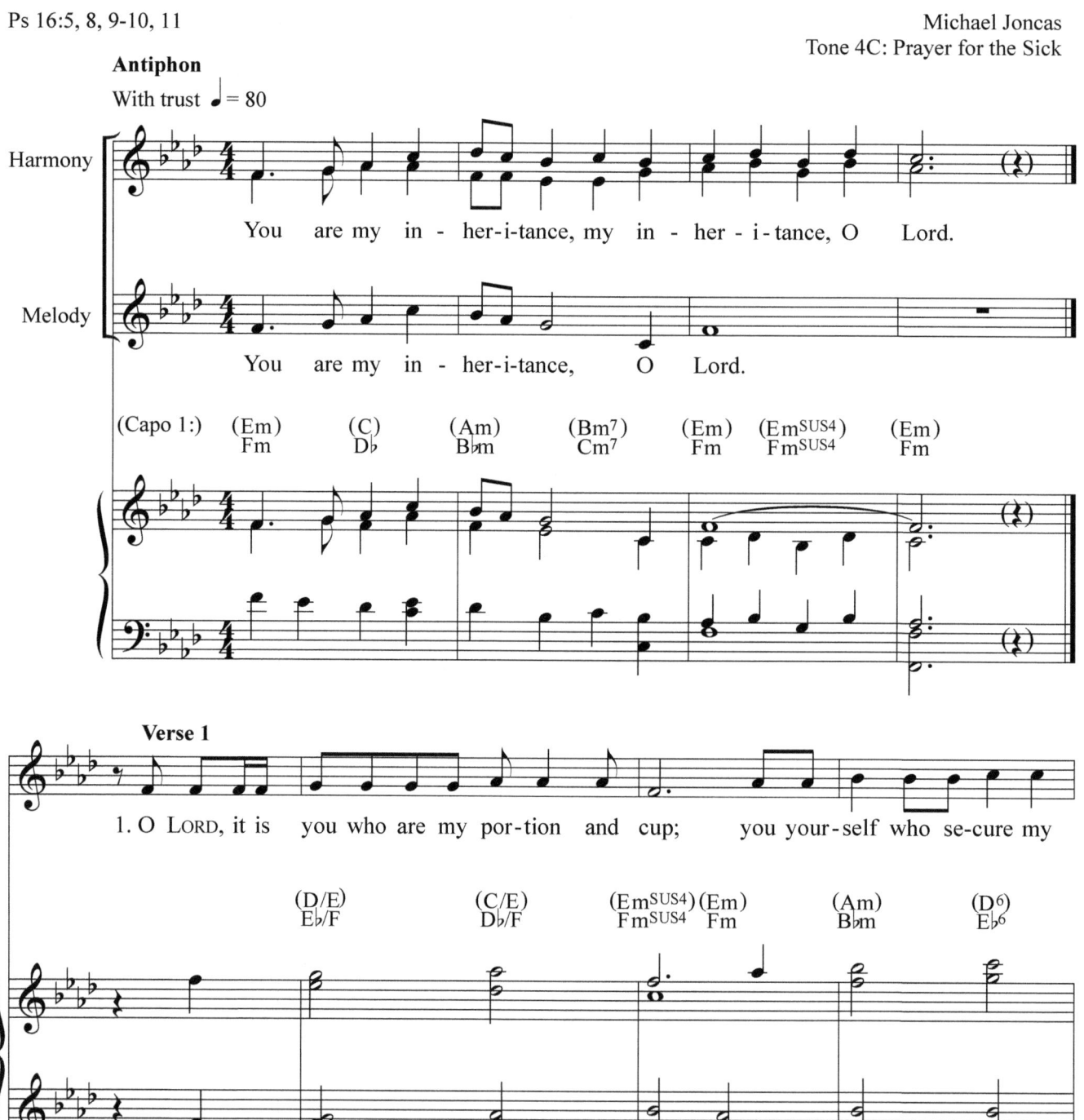

Thirty-Third Sunday in Ordinary Time, Year B

Thirty-Third Sunday in Ordinary Time, Year B

Psalm 93: The Lord Is King

Solemnity of Christ the King/Thirty-Fourth Sunday in Ordinary Time, Year B

Ps 93:1, 1-2, 5

Michael Joncas
Tone 1A: Hymn of Praise,
Motivation from Nature

Solemnity of Christ the King/Thirty-Fourth Sunday in Ordinary Time, Year B

Solemnity of Christ the King/Thirty-Fourth Sunday in Ordinary Time, Year B